American Azaleas

American Azaleas

L. CLARENCE TOWE

Timber Press
Portland ✦ *Cambridge*

Text copyright © 2004 by L. Clarence Towe
Photographs copyright © 2004 by L. Clarence Towe unless otherwise noted
All rights reserved

Published in 2004 by

Timber Press, Inc.
The Haseltine Building
133 S.W. Second Avenue, Suite 450
Portland, Oregon 97204-3527, U.S.A.

Timber Press
2 Station Road
Swavesey
Cambridge CB4 5Q J, U.K.

www.timberpress.com

Printed in Hong Kong

Reprinted 2005

Library of Congress Cataloging-in-Publication Data

Towe, L. Clarence.
        American azaleas / L. Clarence Towe.
            p.   cm.
    Includes bibliographical references (p.   ).
    ISBN 0-88192-645-0 (hardcover)
        1. Azaleas—United States. I. Title.
    SB413.A9T68 2004
    635.9'3366—dc22

2003022318

A catalog record for this book is also available from the British Library.

TO LOUISE, SARAH, JARRETT ROSS, AND JARRETT

Contents

Preface   9

Chapter 1.   Rhododendrons and Azaleas   11
Chapter 2.   American Azaleas   17
Chapter 3.   Collecting Azaleas   39
Chapter 4.   Growing Azaleas   47
Chapter 5.   Landscaping with Azaleas   59
Chapter 6.   Propagating Azaleas   75
Chapter 7.   Improving Azaleas: Past to Present   91
Chapter 8.   Improving Azaleas: Future Possibilities   107
Chapter 9.   Introducing New Azaleas   121

Appendix A.   Azalea Organizations   127
Appendix B.   Azalea Sources   129
Appendix C.   Rhododendron Registration Forms   131
Appendix D.   U.S. Department of Agriculture Hardiness Zones   137
Appendix E.   Metric Equivalents for English Units   139

Bibliography   141
Index   143

Color plates follow page 16

Preface

In 1972 I was given a copy of Fred Galle's first book, *Azaleas*, now worn past the point of usefulness. That gift led to a lifelong interest in American deciduous azaleas, perhaps the most colorful and most misunderstood group of flowering shrubs in North America. At the time I was familiar with two species but quickly found there were seven species in my home state of South Carolina and a record twelve species in neighboring Georgia. I was also surprised to learn that they were classified as rhododendrons, those small trees that line the shady mountain streams I have enjoyed since childhood.

After reading the book I decided to visit the species in their native habitats, all but two of which are located in the southeastern United States. A few years into the project I was joined by Nick Anastos, a mechanic and nurseryman from South Carolina, and later by Ewin Jenkins, an orthopedic surgeon from Alabama. We observed the azaleas closely but took a more casual, tongue-in-cheek attitude toward ourselves and the many interesting people we met along the way. As we traveled we began to notice plants with interesting and unusual traits that seemed to have breeding possibilities. Having closely followed Dr. Richard Jaynes's research in the genus *Kalmia*, it became increasingly clear that manipulating these traits had the potential to give azaleas some of the same types of facelifts he is so successfully giving to mountain laurels.

Azaleas have long been regarded as valuable garden shrubs, but most of the early breeding in Europe, England, and later in the United States focused on increasing flower size. Although some breeding is in progress to develop selections that have increased heat or cold tolerance or bloom later in the season, little true research has been done to uncover the genetics of these colorful members of the rhododendron family.

This book has two purposes. The first is to give the reader an overview of the azalea species of North America and some of their variations and hybrids that can be found in the wild. The second, equally important purpose is to encourage plant breeders to utilize traits that have the potential to bring about fundamental changes in the way these colorful shrubs look, yet allow them to maintain their identity as American azaleas.

Chapter 1

Rhododendrons and Azaleas

To many gardeners the word *azaleas* brings to mind dense evergreen shrubs covered with white, pink, or red flowers. In the Deep South of the United States the word evokes images of sandy drives leading to old plantations surrounded by moss-draped live oaks and tall pines under which azaleas always seem to grow in profusion. As familiar and indispensable as evergreen azaleas are, many who grow them do not know they are of Asian origin and that America has its own azaleas, equally colorful and adaptable to many garden situations. It is also not widely known that deciduous American azaleas, as well as evergreen azaleas, are actually members of the large rhododendron family.

American azaleas are not used enough in landscaping, even in areas where they are common along rural roadsides. In part this is due to the misconception that they will not grow in open residential areas. To make matters worse, many people simply do not know what they are. Even to those who know them, there is confusion and inconsistencies in their common names. They are called deciduous azaleas, native azaleas, or wild azaleas—all perfectly acceptable names—but they are frequently and mistakenly referred to as honeysuckles, bush honeysuckles, or wild honeysuckles. This is probably a result of the similarity of the fragrance and flower shapes of some species of the true honeysuckles of the genus *Lonicera*.

Although they share some similarities with evergreen azaleas, deciduous azaleas have their own distinct characteristics, and trying to explain the differences between the two is not an easy task. As the name implies, deciduous azaleas lose their leaves at the onset of autumn, whereas evergreen azaleas retain approximately half of their leaves during the winter months. If examined closely, perhaps the most conspicuous difference is that deciduous azaleas have two types of buds. In the spring new shoots and leaves emerge from small vegetative buds, whereas flowers (from five to ten per bud) emerge from larger floral buds. In evergreen azaleas, both flowers (one to three per bud) and vegetative shoots originate from the same buds. One important difference that continues to perpetuate the relative obscurity of deciduous azaleas is that they can be difficult to root from softwood cuttings, while evergreen azaleas are very easy to root.

Other differences are subtler. Deciduous azaleas are usually taller, have a more open growth habit with fewer twigs, and are not as densely foliated as evergreen azaleas. Deciduous azaleas also have flowers with long tubes, whereas evergreen azalea flowers have relatively short tubes. The flowers of deciduous azaleas are more in scale to the size of their leaves, while evergreen azaleas have flowers disproportionately larger than their leaves. For example, in some evergreen azaleas such as the low-growing Satsukis, leaves may be only 1 inch long while the flowers may be 3 inches wide. Some deciduous species have bright yellow flowers, a color not found in their evergreen cousins. Several deciduous species are very fragrant, whereas only a few evergreen species are even moderately fragrant. A final difference that often goes unnoticed is that deciduous azaleas shed their flowers quickly after blooming, whereas many evergreen azaleas hold their flowers long after they turn brown.

Classification of Rhododendrons and Azaleas

Genus *Rhododendron*, a term of Greek origin that loosely translates to "rose tree," is one of about 100 genera in the plant family Ericaceae, commonly referred to as the heath family. From a horticultural standpoint, other important heath genera include *Arctostaphylos* (bearberry), *Calluna* (heath), *Erica* (heather), *Kalmia* (laurel), *Leucothoë* (fetter-bush), and *Vaccinium* (blueberries and cranberries). Genus *Rhododendron* contains more than 1000 species, subspecies, and botanical varieties spread across North America, Europe, Asia, and tropical Australasia. Some high-altitude alpine species grow as flattened groundcovers only a few inches tall with half-inch leaves, while some Asian species grow into 100-foot single-trunked trees with 3-foot leaves. In the tropics many *Rhododendron* species are epiphytic and, like orchids, grow on decaying logs and in crevices in rocks and trees.

Rhododendrons have undergone numerous classification changes as taxonomists tried to organize the hundreds of species into logically related categories. Informally, the genus is divided into five groups: lepidote (scaly leaf) rhododendrons, elepidote (nonscaly leaf) rhododendrons, vireya (tropical) rhododendrons, evergreen azaleas, and deciduous azaleas. In 1955, to address the more formal taxonomic issues, the Royal Horticultural Society was named the international registration authority for the genus *Rhododendron* at the 14th International Horticultural Congress. The 1980 edition of their *Rhododendron Handbook* marked the transition to a classification system proposed by Hermann Sleumer in 1949. Since 1980 four international conferences have been held and several experimental techniques have been developed to better classify rhododendrons.

These conferences and studies led to the refined Sleumer Classification System proposed by the Royal Horticultural Society in the 1998 *Rhododendron Handbook*, which divides the genus into seven subgenera, some of which are further divided into sections and subsections.

Genus *Rhododendron*
    Subgenus *Azaleastrum*
    Subgenus *Candidastrum*
    Subgenus *Mumeazalea*
    Subgenus *Pentanthera*
    Subgenus *Rhododendron*
    Subgenus *Therorhodion*
    Subgenus *Tsutsutsi*

The subgenera *Pentanthera* and *Tsutsutsi* contain the rhododendron species classified as azaleas. *Pentanthera* contains only deciduous species, whereas *Tsutsutsi* contains evergreen, semi-evergreen, and deciduous species. Thirteen of the fifteen American species are found in subgenus *Pentanthera*, section *Pentanthera*, subsection *Pentanthera*, which contains fourteen species. They are characterized by having tubular, funnel-shaped flowers and five elongated anthers—hence pentanthera—with several species having conspicuous blotches on their upper petals. (The fourteenth member of this subsection, *Rhododendron luteum*, Pontic azalea, apparently got separated from its relatives and found its way to central Europe, where it is reported to be doing well.) The two other American species, *Rhododendron canadense* and *R. vaseyi*, constitute subgenus *Pentanthera*, section *Pentanthera*, subsection *Rhodora*. From a genetic standpoint they differ considerably from those in subsection *Pentanthera* and from each other. Both have very short tubes flower tubes, split petals, seven to ten anthers instead of five, and speckles instead of blotches on their upper petals.

As now classified, the fifteen American azalea species and their common names are as follows:

Rhododendron alabamense Rehder, Alabama azalea
Rhododendron arborescens (Pursh) Torrey, sweet azalea
Rhododendron atlanticum (Ashe) Rehder, coastal azalea
Rhododendron austrinum (Small) Rehder, Florida azalea
Rhododendron calendulaceum (Michaux) Torrey, flame azalea
Rhododendron canadense (Linnaeus) Torrey, rhodora
Rhododendron canescens (Michaux) Sweet, piedmont azalea
Rhododendron cumberlandense Braun, Cumberland azalea
Rhododendron flammeum (Michaux) Sargent, Oconee azalea
Rhododendron occidentale (Torrey & Gray) Gray, western azalea
Rhododendron periclymenoides (Michaux) Shinners,
    Pinxterbloom azalea
Rhododendron prinophyllum (Small) Millais, roseshell azalea
Rhododendron prunifolium (Small) Millais, plumleaf azalea
Rhododendron vaseyi Gray, pinkshell azalea
Rhododendron viscosum (Linnaeus) Torrey, swamp azalea

The remaining deciduous azalea species are found in Asia. Subgenus *Pentanthera*, section *Pentanthera*, subsection *Sinensia* contains *R. molle*, Chinese azalea, and *R. japonicum*, Japanese azalea, which are very similar to each other and to the thirteen American species in subsection *Pentanthera*. Compared to the American species, they have larger and broader funnel-form flowers, shorter anthers, and speckles instead of blotches on their upper petals.

The four deciduous azaleas in subgenus *Pentanthera*, section *Sciadorho-dion* are *Rhododendron albrechtii*, Albrecht's azalea, *R. pentaphyllum*, five-leaf azalea, and *R. quinquefolium*, cork azalea, all indigenous to Japan, with *R. schlippenbachii*, royal azalea, being found in Korea and Russia. These species have leaves in terminal whorls of five and flowers with ten anthers.

The single deciduous azalea in subgenus *Pentanthera*, section *Viscidula* is *Rhododendron nipponicum*, Nippon azalea, a native of Japan. It has small, pendulous bell-shaped flowers and is considered to be one of the most primitive in the genus.

Subgenus *Tsutsutsi*, section *Tsutsutsi* contains approximately ninety evergreen species. Hybrids among a very few species in this section gave rise to the popular evergreen azaleas we know today. This subgenus, however, has a second division, section *Brachycalyx*, which contains approximately thirty semi-evergreen to deciduous species. Most species in this subsection have leaves in terminal pseudo-whorls of twos and threes and are fully deciduous, whereas some species retain a few of their leaves during the winter months. The most commonly cultivated species are *Rhododendron amagianum*, Mount Amagi azalea, *R. nudipes*, Nudipe azalea, *R. reticulatum*, rose azalea, *R. sanctum*, shrine azalea, *R. wadanum*, Wada's azalea, and *R. weyrichii*, Weyrich azalea. These species are indigenous to Japan. *Rhododendron farrerae*, Farrer azalea, is found in China, and *R. mariesii*, Maries azalea, is found in China and Taiwan. Although these species are deciduous, they are more closely related to evergreen azaleas and have few similarities to American azaleas.

Rhododendron occidentale, western azalea, is one of the most ornamental and temperamental of all American azaleas. This selection has unusually large flowers and dark red foliage. Photograph by Britt Smith

Because *Rhododendron occidentale* does not have yellow flowers, Britt Smith and Frank Mossman decided to create one. They accomplished this in two azalea generations by cross-pollinating plants with yellow pigment in the petals. Photograph by Britt Smith

After many years, *Rhododendron canadense* (rhodora), was finally granted membership into the rhododendron family. The flowers, which have an unusual shape, probably led to the discrimination. Photograph by Russ Hondorf

A lone rhodora is reflected in North Pond at Quaker Hill Native Plant Garden in Pawling, New York. Photograph by Russ Hondorf

White and pink rhodoras add splashes of color to a pondside planting at Quaker Hill. Photograph by Russ Hondorf

Rhododendron vaseyi, pinkshell azalea, has flowers similar to some of its Asian relatives. It is a high-elevation recluse and is one of North America's most attractive species.

A *Rhododendron vaseyi* seedling in Shining Rock Wilderness in North Carolina gives new meaning to being caught between a rock and a hard place.

Rhododendron vaseyi can have red leaves in the summer as well as red fall color.

A group of *Rhododendron vaseyi* keeps a safe distance from the entrance to Devil's Courthouse Tunnel on the Blue Ridge Parkway in North Carolina.

Rhododendron austrinum, Florida azalea, has fragrant yellow flowers and is very easy to grow.

'Millie Mac' is an unusual picotee *Rhododendron austrinum* that has petals with narrow white margins.

This rare yellow-blotched white *Rhododendron austrinum* occasionally produces limbs with bright yellow flowers.

Azaleas are at their best when used as a border between a woodlot and a lawn or driveway. Photograph by Earl Sommerville

A lone *Rhododendron austrinum* greets the morning sun by a pond at Callaway Gardens in Georgia.

A Japanese maple, an American azalea, and a Chinese rhododendron discuss world affairs in Nick Anastos's garden in upstate South Carolina.

Visitors are greeted by azaleas and wildflowers at a lakeside cottage.

Rhododendron austrinum, *R. canescens*, and *R. periclymenoides* bloom early in this hillside garden, their roots warmed by heat from the rock wall and the western exposure.

A backyard garden under tall pines is a low-maintenance way to grow azaleas.

Rhododendron canescens, piedmont azalea, North America's most common species, has a reputation for hybridizing with any nearby partner.

Rhododendron canescens 'Chocolate Drop' has chocolate-red leaves and fragrant white flowers. Photograph by Ernest Koone

A *Rhododendron canescens* seedling displays leaves with strong orange pigmentation.

These azaleas show a part of the hybrid color range between pink *Rhododendron canescens* and orange-to-red *R. flammeum*. Silverbell, *Halesia tetraptera*, is seen in the upper left. Photograph by Ewin Jenkins

Rhododendron flammeum, Oconee azalea, is one of North America's most heat-tolerant species.

The pink pigmentation in this orange *Rhododendron flammeum* suggests it has some *R. canescens* in its family tree.

In full sun *Rhododendron flammeum* produces an abundance of flowers. Photograph by Ewin Jenkins

Rhododendron alabamense, Alabama azalea, has yellow-blotched fragrant white flowers.

A tranquil lakeside scene at Callaway Gardens, Georgia.

Rhododendron eastmanii, May white azalea, is a putative new yellow-blotched fragrant white species that has been verified in several counties in South Carolina. Photograph by Mike Creel

Rhododendron atlanticum, coastal azalea, spreads by underground stolons to form large colonies of a single plant. Photograph by Earl Sommerville

Rhododendron atlanticum (f. *polypetala*) has narrow straplike petals. Photograph by Mike Creel

Rhododendron periclymenoides, Pinxterbloom azalea, is a widespread fragrant pink species that is hardy and easy to grow.

A fifty-year-old *Rhododendron periclymenoides* in upstate South Carolina watches over the pasture every afternoon until the cows come home.

Rhododendron prinophyllum, roseshell azalea, has bright pink flowers with a distinct spicy fragrance.

Dolly Sods Wilderness in West Virginia is one of the best areas to see *Rhododendron prinophyllum*. Photograph by Steve Hootman

Interesting things happen when *Rhododendron periclymenoides* hybridizes with *R. calendulaceum*. 'Magic Pink' opens light pink and changes to bright red.

A *Rhododendron calendulaceum* × *R. canescens* hybrid, 'Doctor Helen', opens white and then turns bright rose. Photograph by Ewin Jenkins

These *Rhododendron calendulaceum* × *R. periclymenoides* hybrids were found in a small area near Lake Keowee in South Carolina.

'Keowee Sunset', a *Rhododendron calendulaceum* × *R. periclymenoides* hybrid, respectfully combines the colors of its parents.

Flowers with ruffled petal margins are one indicator of hybridization.

Flowers with more than five petals are also an indicator of hybridization.

'Gamecock' has narrow featherlike petals.

Rhododendron calendulaceum, flame azalea, is the species most frequently associated with the Appalachian Mountains.

The flowers of *Rhododendron calendulaceum* are usually orange to orange-red in color but plants with clear yellow and bright red flowers can be found.

Rhododendron calendulaceum thrives in rugged mountain terrain.

Mountain architecture is at its best in this ranger station along the Blue Ridge Parkway in Virginia: split shingles, weathered siding, granite stepping-stones, and a single azalea for color.

Azaleas greet visitors at Brasstown Bald Observation Tower in northern Georgia.

Many observers consider Roan Mountain along the North Carolina–Tennessee border to be the premiere azalea site in North America.

Rhododendron calendulaceum in front of purple rhododendrons (*R. catawbiense*) and spruce trees (*Picea rubens*).

The Appalachian Trail winds through grassy meadows and thickets of azaleas and rhododendrons as it crosses Round Bald in the Roan Highlands.

Clearcutting, despite its drawbacks, allows azaleas an opportunity to regain their vigor. The forgetful logger left some of his firewood.

An orange *Rhododendron calendulaceum* has little trouble making its presence known among light pink mountain laurels.

If this azalea is not rescued soon, wave action will undercut the bank, sending it into the lake below. Despite the dry site and shallow soil, it is in a vigorous state of growth.

These flowers represent only a small part of the color range of *Rhododendron calendulaceum*.

An eastern tiger swallowtail butterfly is attracted to a *Rhododendron calendulaceum* near Mount Mitchell, North Carolina.

Rhododendron cumberlandense, Cumberland azalea, from the Talladega Mountains in Alabama has glossier foliage than those from the northern end of the species' range in Kentucky.

Azaleas and split-rail fences go together like ham and eggs.

The small, fleshy flowers of this *Rhododendron cumberlandense* mutation resemble tiny banana peels and may be a new and unreported flower type in azaleas.

Allen Cantrell found this double *Rhododendron cumberlandense* in northern Georgia. The light areas on the leaves are a symptom of iron chlorosis, a problem that can be solved with a mild application of azalea fertilizer.

Variegated foliage is rare in azaleas, but the trait can be attractive in its better expressions.

This *Rhododendron cumberlandense* hybrid has the potential to lead to a new line of compact azaleas.

Rhododendron viscosum, swamp azalea, has white flowers with very sticky tubes that frequently trap small insects.

Compact *Rhododendron viscosum* (var. *montanum*) is found on high mountaintops and has glossy foliage and small flowers.

Rhododendron arborescens, sweet azalea, has fragrant white flowers with red pistils and filaments. It is frequently confused with swamp azalea, *R. viscosum*.

A rare yellow *Rhododendron arborescens*.

Rhododendron arborescens frequently hybridizes with *R. calendulaceum*, usually producing pastel orange flowers with red tubes.

Wayah Bald in western North Carolina is topped with dense thickets of *Rhododendron arborescens*.

Rhododendron arborescens grows with a small rhododendron by a trout stream in North Carolina.

'Millennium' is a *Rhododendron arborescens* hybrid with fragrant red flowers and glossy, blue-green foliage.

'Mountain Creek White', a *Rhododendron arborescens* × *R. viscosum* hybrid, combines the best traits of both parents. Note the dark green foliage and tubular flowers.

A pink *Rhododendron arborescens* hybrid dares to be different by displaying white blotches instead of the usual yellow or orange ones.

Rhododendron prunifolium, plumleaf azalea, usually blooms in August, long after the flowers of most azaleas have disappeared.

Providence Canyon in Georgia is home to ravine-dwelling plumleaf azalea.

Azaleas grow along a narrow border near the floor of Providence Canyon.

Rows of micropropagated spring liners at Lazy K Nursery in Georgia will grow fast their first summer and some will bloom the following year.

In colder climates open shade-houses should be covered with white plastic to provide protection from winter damage.

Azalea flower buds from several species and hybrids show considerable variation in size, shape, and color.

Variation in size and vigor is common in hybrid azalea seedlings.

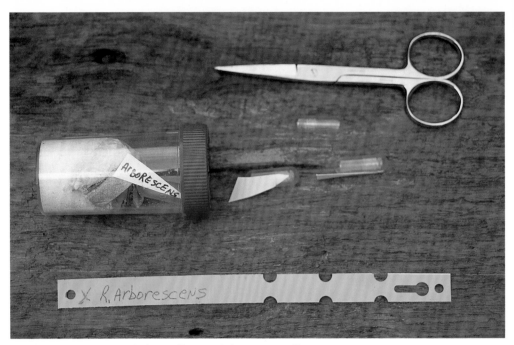

The equipment needed to collect and desiccate pollen is easy to use.

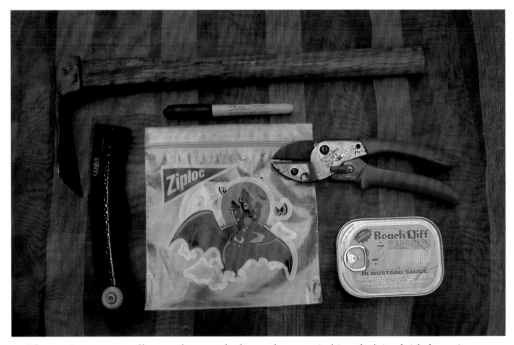

The equipment to collect azaleas works best when carried in a lady's plaid shopping bag. Lunch is on your own.

Chapter 2

American Azaleas

While the botanical names and numbers of species of American azaleas have changed over the years, it is now generally recognized that there are fifteen species in North America. Although centered in the United States, one eastern species crosses northward into Canada and one species is found in a small area south of the border in northwestern Mexico. In the past, several authorities attempted to lump American azaleas (hereafter "azaleas") into alliances by correlating biochemical analyses with morphological characteristics. Due to different approaches and interpretations of data, these attempts failed to conclusively resolve the many relationships that exist between the species.

The group approach used here is not an attempt to revisit alliances or to add further layers of taxonomy but is intended to present the species in a practical manner. Each group contains a number of species equal to the group number. The groups are based on geographical isolation in one instance, lack of fragrance in another, and fragrance or similar colors in others. The descriptions are composites as noted by several authorities and based on personal observations of readily observable characteristics across the ranges of the species. Within each group the species are listed in order of bloom time.

In keeping with international rules of plant nomenclature, the names of some species were changed to the names first referenced in early literature. While this gives credit where due, it has led to some confusion, and several species are still referred to by their old names. *Rhododendron specio-*

sum was changed to *R. flammeum*, a very descriptive name for the bright orange and red flowers of this lowland species. The change, however, has led to some confusion because the common name of *R. calendulaceum* is flame azalea. *Rhododendron nudiflorum*, a name any azalea would aspire to, was changed to the tongue-twisting *R. periclymenoides*. *Rhododendron roseum*, a perfectly descriptive name, was changed to *R. prinophyllum*, which sounds much like *R. prunifolium*. *Rhododendron bakeri* was changed to *R. cumberlandense* to reflect its Cumberland Plateau range in the southern Appalachian Mountains.

Within the species, many botanical varieties (var.) and forms (f.) were recognized at one time, but most of these infraspecies names were dropped as the species became better understood. Rules of plant nomenclature invalidated some infraspecies names still in use today, which creates a problem in referencing them in an acceptable manner. One taxonomist suggests parentheses as a means to describe plants with unique qualities but that may be invalid from a taxonomic standpoint. For example, *Rhododendron arborescens* (var. *georgiana*) will be used here to denote the late-blooming southern form of *R. arborescens*.

The distribution maps present approximate ranges, and in any area azaleas have uneven distributions. Some large areas within a range may be devoid of azaleas, whereas other areas may be heavily populated. In actuality it is likely that all ranges are larger than depicted on the distribution maps. Hardiness within each species is also variable, and hardiness zones should be used only as guides (for temperature ranges of hardiness zones, see Appendix D). For example, plants from the southern end of the range of *Rhododendron viscosum*, which spreads from the Gulf of Mexico into New England, are not as hardy as plants from the northern end of the range.

In discussing azaleas a few botanical terms can be helpful to develop a better understanding of how they are divided into species. The primary species indicators are bloom time, flower color and fragrance, leaf shape and texture, and the presence or absence of small hairs on new stems, leaves, bud scales, and flower parts. These hairs may be slender and unicellular or thick and multicellular. Multicellular hairs are usually tipped with sticky or nonsticky knoblike glands. A plant part lacking hairs or having only a few scattered hairs is glabrous; one covered with hairs is pubescent. Leaves covered with a waxy white, gray, or blue powder are said to be glaucous, and a plant that spreads by underground runners is stolonifereous. Leaf shapes can be elliptical (widest in the center) or obovate (widest near the tip).

Group One

This group consists of one species, *Rhododendron occidentale*, western azalea, a geographically isolated species with a range from southern Oregon, across California, and into a small area in northwestern Mexico (see Figure 1). It grows at low elevations along the Pacific coastline to as high as 8000 feet in coniferous forests on the western slopes of the Sierra Nevada. In its typical form the relatively small fragrant white, cream, or pale pink flowers have yellow blotches. The flower tubes, petal ribs, leaf margins, and seedpods are covered with conspicuous glandular hairs, a trait shared with a few East Coast species.

Leaves are usually 3 inches or less in length, and upper surfaces vary from smooth to very hairy. Growth habit varies from low and stoloniferous to more than 30 feet in height, making it North America's tallest azalea. Scattered among these typical forms are plants with unusually large flowers, frequently to 3 inches and occasionally to 4 inches. The petals are wide and overlapping, with some having crimped or frilled margins and velvety, creped surfaces. Colors vary from light pink to deep pink to pinkish red to red, occasionally with red picotee margins, and most have yellow or orange speckles instead of blotches in the throats.

A puzzling aspect of this species is its reluctance to grow and thrive on the East Coast. It will grow here for some time but in due course usually declines and dies. Even in areas with microclimates similar to the West Coast, *Rhododendron occidentale* seldom lives more than a few years. One theory is that soil chemistry, rather than climate, restricts its growth on the East Coast. Bloom time is from May to August, and it is hardy from zones 7 to 9.

Several noted authorities have speculated that *Rhododendron occidentale* may have resulted from the assimilation of two or even three ancestral species into one highly variable species. While leaves are usually 3 inches or less in length, some can be up to 6 inches in length, and the large-flowered forms have either speckles on the upper petals or large

Figure 1. Distribution range of *Rhododendron occidentale*. Drawing by Allen Cantrell

blotches that break up into speckles around the blotch margins. These foliage and flower traits are also found on *R. molle* and *R. japonicum*, located across the Pacific Ocean in eastern China and Japan. Theories of continental drift place North America and Asia in close proximity in past millennia, raising the possibility that these similarities may be more than coincidental.

Group Two

This group contains two nonfragrant pink species, *Rhododendron canadense* and *R. vaseyi*. Unlike other azaleas, which have five anthers, these two species have from seven to ten anthers and are not closely related to each other or to any other azalea species. Their respective distribution ranges are shown in Figure 2.

Rhodora, *Rhododendron canadense*, is found in low-lying glaciated areas of New Jersey, Pennsylvania, New York, throughout New England, and into eastern Canada. The tubeless flowers have from seven to ten anthers. The three upper petals are fused into one speckled petal with three marginal lobes, and the two lower petals are narrow and widely splayed. Flower color ranges from white (rarely) to lavender-pink to vivid pinkish purple. The glaucous leaves are small and grayish green with slightly raspy surfaces, although in a few areas plants have been found with smooth, bright green leaves. Rhodora is a low-growing (3-foot) plant capable of spreading long distances by underground stolons. Bloom time is from April to May, and it is hardy from zones 3 to 6.

Pinkshell azalea, *Rhododendron vaseyi*, is a reclusive high-elevation species whose range is restricted to seven counties in western North Carolina and one county in northeastern Georgia. It prefers rich, damp, well-drained soil and cooler summer temperatures than most azalea species. It is usually found from 4000 to 6000 feet above sea level and can languish at lower elevations if summer heat is excessive. *Rhododendron vaseyi* is an open-growing, weakly branched shrub with smooth stems covered with shreddy, gray-brown bark. The flowers have seven anthers, short glabrous tubes, and deeply divided petals that appear just before or with the emerging foliage, giving a bare plant the look of being covered with pink butterflies. Flower color ranges from white (rarely) with green speckles in

Figure 2. Distribution range of (A) *Rhododendron canadense* and (B) *R. vaseyi*.
Drawing by Allen Cantrell

the throats to light pink to vivid pink with reddish throat speckles. Winter buds are fat and plump, with a shape unlike any other species. Terminal leaves are smooth and narrowly elliptical, whereas leaves on lower limbs are more obovate. If exposed to full sun, leaves can be wine red during most of the year. Fall leaf color varies from red to yellow, depending on sun exposure and night temperatures. Bloom time in its home range is from early to late May, and it is hardy from zones 4 to 7.

Group Three

This group contains three fragrant pink species, *Rhododendron canescens*, *R. periclymenoides*, and *R. prinophyllum*. Their respective distribution ranges are shown in Figure 3.

Piedmont azalea, *Rhododendron canescens*, is our most common species. It is found primarily in the Deep South and is closely related to its more northern counterparts, *R. periclymenoides* and *R. prinophyllum*. *Rhododendron canescens* is a tall (15-foot) nonstoloniferous shrub found in a variety of locations, from damp swamp margins to dry upland ridges. The flowers are typically white to light pink with pink tubes, but bright pink forms exist. Flower fragrance is sweet to musky sweet. The flower tubes are covered with both glandular and nonglandular hairs. The medium green obovate leaves are usually dull, due to being covered with short, raspy hairs above and with dense, downy hairs below. Floral bud scales are pearlescent, which adds to the overall canescent (dusty) look of the plant and gives rise to one of its more obscure names, hoary azalea. Bloom time is from March to early May, and it is hardy from zones 6 to 9.

Pinxterbloom azalea, *Rhododendron periclymenoides*, overlaps the northern end of the range of *R. canescens* and extends northward into southern New England. Its growth habit varies from low and stoloniferous to upright to 12 feet, and it is usually found in fairly dry soil in open hardwood forests. Flower color varies from pure white (rarely) to pale pink to bright purplish violet, with most flowers having dark pink to strawberry red tubes. Typically the flower tubes are covered with nonglandular hairs, in contrast to the glandular hairs of *R. canescens* and *R. prinophyllum*. The flowers occasionally have wide petals but are more often

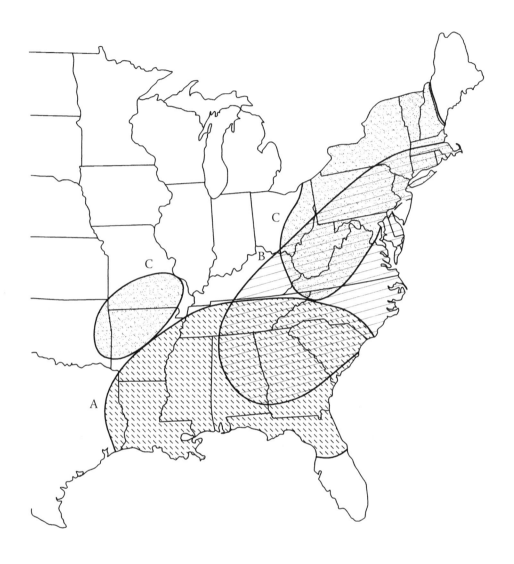

Figure 3. Distribution range of (A) *Rhododendron canescens*,
(B) *R. periclymenoides*, and (C) *R. prinophyllum*. Drawing by Allen Cantrell

narrow and twisted, giving them a frazzled, wind-blown look. When present, fragrance is moderately musky sweet. Leaves are generally smooth and semiglossy on top and from elliptical to obovate in shape. The Pinxterbloom azalea hybridizes readily with *R. canescens* to the south and *R. prinophyllum* to the north, creating a huge swath of fragrant pink azaleas inside a triangle from Florida to Texas to New Hampshire. Bloom time is from April to May, and it is hardy from zones 4 to 8.

Roseshell azalea, *Rhododendron prinophyllum*, differs in several respects from its two fragrant pink relatives. Its primary range is in the cooler upland and mountainous areas of Virginia and West Virginia, across Pennsylvania and upstate New York, and into New England. Oddly, is has a disjunct range west of the Mississippi River in southern Missouri, Arkansas, and eastern Oklahoma. The plants are usually nonstoloniferous and moderate in height (to 8 feet). The flowers have shorter tubes than the two other fragrant pink species, the tubes are covered with moderately sticky glands, and the fragrance is sweet and clovelike. Flower color varies from pale pink to vivid pink to violet-pink, with many having darker pink elliptical blotches on the upper petals. The petals can be narrow or relatively wide, usually with dark pink to strawberry red tubes. Emerging leaves are coppery in color and have impressed veins, causing them to have lumpy upper surfaces. They are also covered with soft hairs, giving rise to one of its older common names, downy azalea. Due to its preference for the cooler mountains, it has also been called mountain pink azalea in some areas. Bloom time is from May to June, and it is hardy from zones 4 to 8.

Group Four

This group contains four fragrant white species, *Rhododendron alabamense*, *R. atlanticum*, *R. arborescens*, and *R. viscosum*. Their respective distribution ranges are shown in Figure 4.

Alabama azalea, *Rhododendron alabamense*, is found primarily in Alabama, but crosses into central Tennessee to the north and is found sporadically across Georgia to the east, in a small area of the Florida panhandle to the south, and west into Mississippi. Although the distribution range is fairly large, *R. alabamense* is not a common species. It was proba-

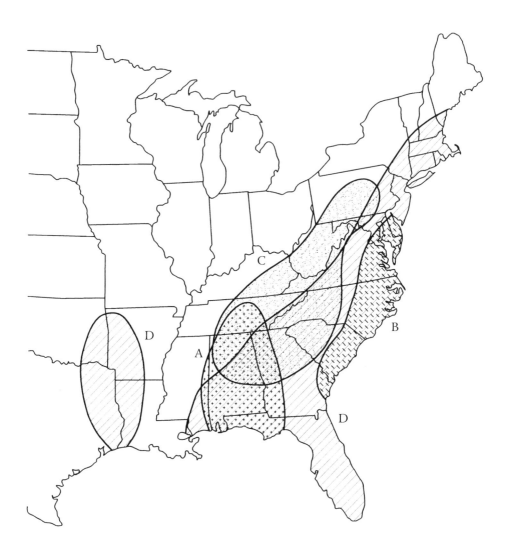

Figure 4. Distribution range of (A) *Rhododendron alabamense*,
(B) *R. atlanticum*, (C) *R. arborescens*, and (D) *R. viscosum*. Drawing by
Allen Cantrell

bly more widely distributed in the past, but hybridization with *R. canescens* may have assimilated it into that species complex in many areas. In its better forms it is very attractive. It is found along dry ridges and steep bluffs, as well as in flat, moist, sandy areas. The plants vary from low and stoloniferous to upright to 12 feet. The flowers have a sweet or musky-sweet scent, frequently with distinct lemon overtones. Flower color is white to white with yellow blotches, while some are flushed pink. The flower tubes are covered with glandular and nonglandular hairs, making them moderately sticky. Leaf surfaces vary from semiglossy to dull and from dark to medium green in color. Like its relative *R. arborescens*, many plants of this species have dark green leaves that are glaucous underneath and fragrant when crushed. Bloom time is from late April to early June, and it is hardy from zones 6 to 8.

Coastal azalea, *Rhododendron atlanticum*, is a low-growing species found from Delaware south to Georgia, and up to 200 miles inland in sandy coastal plains along damp ditches, sandy swamp margins, and in dry pasture sites. If the soil is loose *R. atlanticum* will spread by underground stolons, forming large colonies of a single plant. The fragrant flowers are typically white, often flushed pink. Flower tubes are very glandular and can be white or pink, and occasionally plants are found with pale yellow or pale pink flowers. Leaves are usually glaucous gray-green or blue-green, frequently with good substance. Bloom time is from April to May, and it is hardy from zones 5 to 8.

Sweet azalea, *Rhododendron arborescens*, is found along fast-moving streams and damp mountaintops from Alabama to Pennsylvania. It is usually tightly stoloniferous and can form dense clumps to 15 feet in height. The fragrant white flowers (rarely light pink or light yellow) often have yellow blotches and are fairly large, frequently exceeding 2 inches in width. Flowers typically have red pistils and filaments, making *R. arborescens* one of North America's most distinct species. Most flowers have white tubes, but some have light green or pink tubes. Leaves are smooth and glossy to semiglossy and vary in color from medium to dark green to glaucous blue-green with white undersides. New growth is smooth and hairless, giving rise to its other name, smooth azalea. Crushed or dried leaves and twigs are almost always fragrant. Unlike its relatives, *R. arborescens* has granular seeds instead of winged seeds. Bloom time is from May to August, and it is hardy from zones 5 to 8.

In the past the sweet azalea has been credited with two botanical varieties. *Rhododendron arborescens* (var. *richardsonii*) was described as being a low, stoloniferous plant with blue-green foliage. In actuality plants that fit this description are fairly common in the Appalachian Mountains, and they appear to be hybrids with low-growing, high-elevation plants of *R. viscosum*. Another form that is not well known is (var. *georgiana*). This low-elevation form, found in Alabama, Georgia, and Mississippi, differs from typical *R. arborescens* in several ways. It has dark green leaves that are not fragrant when crushed, and the leaves are not glaucous. Another difference is that it blooms in August and September instead of May through July, like its upland counterpart. The fragrant flowers have typical red pistils and filaments, seldom with yellow blotches, and the growth habit is nonstoloniferous.

Swamp azalea, *Rhododendron viscosum*, covers a large distribution area. When examined across its range, it is North America's most variable species. East of the Mississippi River it is found along coastal areas from Mississippi to Florida and up the East Coast as far as southern Maine. It is also found 400 miles inland in some high-elevation areas in the southern Appalachians. West of the Mississippi River it is found in Missouri, eastern Oklahoma, eastern Texas, and northern Louisiana. *Rhododendron viscosum* seldom grows along fast-moving streams like *R. arborescens*, instead preferring damp ditches, swamp margins, sandy fields, and dry ridges. Leaf shape varies from small and narrow to large and rounded, and leaf color varies from dull gray-green to glossy dark green to glaucous gray-green or blue-green. Leaf texture can be raspy or smooth. Although distinct, *R. viscosum* is most often confused with *R. arborescens*, but the two can be separated by touch alone. The new stems of *R. viscosum* are slender and hairy, whereas the new stems of *R. arborescens* are larger and smooth. *Rhododendron viscosum* has slender tubes and fragrant white flowers (rarely pink) that are small to medium in size with narrow to medium width petals. Pistils and filaments are typically white, in contrast to the red pistils of *R. arborescens*. This species has two other common names, catch-fly azalea and clammy azalea, both attributable to its sticky, glandular tube hairs that easily trap flying insects. Bloom time is from May to September and it is hardy from zones 4 to 9.

Rhododendron viscosum is frequently referenced as having two botanical varieties. The low-growing, high-elevation type (var. *montanum*) resembles its low-country counterpart (var. *aemulans*). Due to the seamless range of plant heights found in this species—from very low to very tall—it is doubtful these epithets meet the taxonomic standard for varietal status.

As now classified, dwarf *Rhododendron coryi*, *R. oblongifolium*, Texas azalea, and *R. serrulatum*, hammock-sweet azalea, have been lumped with *R. viscosum*. There are those who insist, however, that *R. serrulatum* is distinct enough to remain at the species level. It is one of the earliest azaleas to leaf out in the spring, much earlier than *R. viscosum*, and the shiny leaves and new stems frequently contain strong red pigmentation. It also has small bud scales that may be very red during the winter months. From a horticultural, if not taxonomic standpoint, it deserves the status of *R. viscosum* (var. *serrulatum*).

Group Five

This group contains five yellow, orange, and red species, *Rhododendron austrinum*, *R. flammeum*, *R. calendulaceum*, *R. cumberlandense*, and *R. prunifolium*. Their respective distribution ranges are shown in Figure 5.

Florida azalea, *Rhododendron austrinum,* is probably distressed to be lumped with its four nonfragrant relatives. It is most closely related to *R. canescens*, and when they are not in bloom the two are very difficult to separate. It is found in the Florida panhandle, southern Georgia and Alabama, and southeastern Mississippi. This colorful species is early to bloom and easy to grow, making it one of North America's most popular species. The fragrant yellow, gold, or light orange flowers usually have pink to strawberry red tubes, which may be a result of hybridization with *R. canescens*. Flower tubes are glandular, as are leaves and new stems. Mature leaves are usually obovate and covered with short, raspy hairs. The growth habit is nonstoloniferous to 15 feet. *Rhododendron austrinum* thrives in the sand and heat of its Gulf Coast range. Bloom time is from March to April, and it is hardy from zones 6 to 9.

Oconee azalea, *Rhododendron flammeum*, discovered along the Oconee River in Georgia, is not a well-known or widely grown species. It is usually nonstoloniferous and grows to 6 to 8 feet tall. It is heat tolerant and exhibits a wide range of bright colors from yellow to orange to red. Flowers emerge with the leaves, which are usually dark green and shiny when

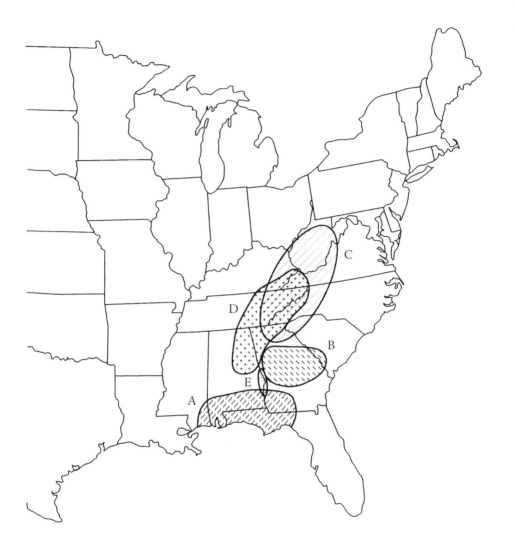

Figure 5. Distribution range of (A) *Rhododendron austrinum*,
(B) *R. flammeum*, (C) *R. calendulaceum*, (D) *R. cumberlandense*, and
(E) *R. prunifolium*. Drawing by Allen Cantrell

young. In the wild it hybridizes freely with *R. canescens*, giving rise to vivid pinks, frequently with yellow blotches. *Rhododendron flammeum* is often confused with *R. calendulaceum*, though the former has nonglandular flower tubes in contrast to glandular flower tubes of the latter. Bloom time is from April to early May, and it is hardy from zones 6 to 8.

Flame azalea, *Rhododendron calendulaceum*, is the azalea most frequently associated with the Appalachian Mountains, and many consider it to be the most attractive eastern species. It begins blooming at 800 feet in the upper piedmont of the South and finishes its season at more than 6000 feet in the Appalachian Mountains. It is a tall, nonstoloniferous shrub that can grow to 12 feet. Flower color varies from yellow to orange to red, with many forms having orange blotches and slight pink overtones. Two-inch flowers are common, and some can be found to 3 inches in width. Flower petals vary from narrow with pointed tips to wide and overlapping with rounded tips. Flower tubes are glandular, in contrast to the three other orange-red azaleas in this group. Bloom time is from April to July, and it is hardy from zones 5 to 8.

Cumberland azalea, *Rhododendron cumberlandense*, is another high-elevation orange-to-red species that is easy to confuse with *R. calendulaceum* and *R. flammeum*. Like *R. flammeum*, it has sparse, nonglandular tube hairs, but its leaves are fully expanded when the flowers appear and it blooms several weeks later. It differs from *R. calendulaceum*, which blooms with or just after the leaves have expanded, by having smaller flowers with thinner tubes. Plants are typically low and twiggy, but they can grow to 10 feet. Leaves emerge late in the season and have smooth, semi-glossy to glossy surfaces, frequently glaucous underneath. Along overlap areas between their ranges, *R. cumberlandense* and *R. calendulaceum* have hybridized and the plants are very difficult to identify. Bloom time is from May to July, and it is hardy from zones 4 to 8.

Plumleaf azalea, *Rhododendron prunifolium*, has orange-red to red flowers but is very different from the others in this group. As in *R. arborescens*, the leaves and new stems are smooth. The dark green leaves emerge very early in the season and are relatively large. The flower tubes are also glabrous, or nearly so, a unique trait that helps with identification. It is a tall shrub, up to 20 feet or more, and prefers cool ravines and creeksides in its small eleven-county range along the Alabama-Georgia border. Due to its late bloom time, this species is very stable, though some plants have pinkish or salmon flowers, perhaps indicating past hybridization with nearby *R. arborescens* (var. *georgiana*). Bloom time is from July to September, and it is hardy from zones 6 to 9.

A New Species?

In the early 1980s, Charles Eastman, a highway engineer and birdwatcher, noticed a fragrant white azalea at Santee State Park in South Carolina. *Rhododendron alabamense* had been identified in South Carolina years earlier, but he became convinced it was a similar but different species. At some point Eastman contacted Mike Creel with the South Carolina Department of Natural Resources, who was also familiar with azaleas. Mike and Charles visited the site several times and both became convinced it was not *R. alabamense*. Mike succeeded in enlisting the support of Kathleen Kron, professor of botany at Wake Forest University in North Carolina. At first she was doubtful, but Mike's persistence convinced her to visit the site; after extensive laboratory analysis, she too became convinced. The new azalea was named *R. eastmanii* to honor its finder, with the common name of May white azalea, due to it being the only white species that blooms in that area in May. The following is based on Mike Creel's description of *R. eastmanii*.

America's newest azalea species, *Rhododendron eastmanii*, commonly known as May white azalea, was initially found growing in two widely separated South Carolina counties, Richland in the lower piedmont and Orangeburg in the middle coastal plain. It has recently been confirmed in five new sites—mostly on steep north-facing circumneutral bluffs—in Calhoun, Laurens, Newberry, Union, and York Counties. Still to be investigated are suspect herbarium specimens and reported sightings in Aiken, Berkley, Dorchester, and Spartanburg Counties.

Critical characters for *R. eastmanii* include: mid-May bloom time, fully expanded and mature stems and leaves at bloom time, a truss of yellow-blotched white flowers with few or no sticky tube glands, a habitat of circumneutral soils and often steep north-facing bluffs, and the strong pleasant fragrance that carries for an extended distance. In addition technical characteristics of flower buds in identifying nonflowering and dormant plants are helpful later in the season, as well as herbarium specimens. While the vegetative bud scales are glabrous abaxially, with unicellular ciliate margins, the flower buds are perhaps the most distinctive feature for plants not in bloom. Flower bud scales are edged chestnut brown; the abaxial surface is glabrous; and the margins are unicellular-ciliate near the apex, glandular along the lower two-thirds. This character seems unique to the species. Such nonmorphological characters as floral fragrance and phenology are also important. Field observations show that *R. eastmanii* is characterized by its distinctive strong, fresh smell, which is different from any other southeastern species. If fragrance in flowers could be shared, its aroma would be a worthy subject as it has the most profound perfume of all. In addition it flowers during the second and third weeks in May, a time when no other native azalea is blooming.

Because of its flower color and fragrance it may be possible to confuse *Rhododendron eastmanii* with *R. alabamense*; however, some specific differences separate the two species. *Rhododendron alabamense* flowers before the leaves have expanded, and flower bud scales lack marginal glands. In contrast, flower bud scales of *R. eastmanii* have marginal glands and the leaves are fully expanded before the flowers open. The fragrance of the two species also differs: *R. alabamense* has a lighter and sweeter quality to its fragrance than *R. eastmanii*. Both species can be found on limestone, but *R. eastmanii* is apparently more consistently associated with nearly neutral soils than is *R. alabamense*, which tolerates a wider range of soils.

A study begun in 2001 is being conducted by the Wildlife Diversity Section of the South Carolina Department of Natural Resources on plant species of federal concern in calcareous and chert formations of the South Carolina coastal plain. *Rhododendron eastmanii* is one of the nine target species that state botanists are seeking within the study. A number of counties in South Carolina where soils with circumneutral pH reactions of 6.0 to 6.7 along bluffs are now known to exist and offer the potential for populations of the new azalea to be discovered.

Rhododendron eastmanii has significant potential for native landscape design because of its appearance, fragrance, and tolerance of less acidic soils than many rhododendrons. It could be of additional value in plant breeding due to its apparent lime tolerance, propensity to bloom well in the shade, unique bloom time, and pleasant fragrance. Individuals interested in the technical aspects of *R. eastmanii* can refer to the article where it was first described (Kron and Creel 1999). This article contains detailed botanical drawings to aid in precise identification.

RHODODENDRON EASTMANII: A SECOND OPINION

Some who follow azaleas closely were skeptical when Kron and Creel's findings were published. Mike, a long-time friend, and I discussed the plant often during the time it was being considered for species status. Nick Anastos, Ewin Jenkins, and I first saw the new azalea in May 2000 in an area that contains about 300 plants. The fragrant flowers exhibited subtle but significant degrees of variation. Corolla color ranged from solid white to white with pale yellow or bright yellow blotches. Pistil and filament color ranged from white to light pink. Leaves were dark green with dull to semiglossy glabrous surfaces and stems were moderately hairy. A few plants, however, had glossy dark green leaves, smooth stems, and red pistils, three traits usually associated with *Rhododendron arborescens*. The plants were growing on the edges of dry bluffs as well as within a few inches of the slow-moving stream that bisects the site.

One way to determine if a new plant is a species is to first rule out the possibility that it is a hybrid. Of the numerous hybrid swarms we have observed, they always grow in close proximity to at least two parental species that bloom at the same time. At one site, we found one *Rhododendron canescens* that had bloomed a few weeks earlier. It has also been reported that no other species near this site blooms in May, though *R. canescens*, *R. periclymenoides*, and *R. viscosum* have been found in close proximity to *R. eastmanii* at other sites.

With no potential parental species in bloom nearby, ongoing hybridization as an explanation begins to fade from the picture. Other factors, however, present evidence that the plant may be of hybrid origin, as many species probably are. Kron noted that some flowers had calyxes with uneven sepal lengths and we found plants with flowers with six petals—two traits associated with hybridization. We also found plants with compact, contorted growth habits, a trait not typically associated with a stable species. Again, as noted by Kron, the plants had glands present along the lower two-thirds of bud scale margins, but this trait has since been observed in other species and wild hybrids.

Other issues add to the mystery. In the 1950s Fred Galle found fragrant white azaleas on the northern slope of Pine Mountain in Georgia in terrain similar to the *Rhododendron eastmanii* sites, and he moved several to Callaway Gardens. The plants have white flowers with yellow blotches, and they bloom after new growth has hardened. Though they bloom a few days later than other plants of this species in the garden, Galle identified them as *R. alabamense*. Similar azaleas with yellow-blotched white flowers emerging after new growth hardens have been grown in private gardens in Alabama for years, where they are referred to as *R. alabamense*. Collectors there have noted that *R. alabamense* blooms from late April to late May, occasionally into early June, and that the later forms have fully expanded leaves and shoots at bloom time.

When all the evidence is examined, the question is whether *Rhododendron eastmanii* is a new species, an azalea of recent hybrid origin on the verge of speciation, *R. alabamense*, or disjunct populations of *R. viscosum* (var. *oblongifolium*). One of the earmarks of a species is that it will duplicate itself when self-pollinated. If a plant is of hybrid origin, self-pollinated seedlings will exhibit a morphological range with some resembling both parental species. This experiment could shed some light on the issue. Plants within a species also have a familial look, even considering inevitable variations. To the layman, *R. eastmanii* looks like the late-blooming forms of *R. alabamense* found in Alabama, Georgia, and Tennessee, and comparisons should be made among specimens from these sites. Another possibility is that the late-blooming whites in these states are actually *R. eastmanii*. Whatever the outcome, this putative new species deserves a chance to conclusively validate its status by being subjected to these and other evaluations before the book is closed on the issue.

Wild Hybrid Azaleas

As discussed here, a hybrid is an azalea resulting from cross-pollination between azaleas of two or more species. On the East Coast twelve of the fourteen azalea species will hybridize naturally. Due to bloom times and distribution ranges as they now exist, however, several species are isolated geographically and have no opportunities to hybridize. The issue of frequency of hybridization in the wild is controversial. Some suggest that hybridization is relatively rare, whereas others feel that all azaleas are hybrids. As is the case with most divergent opinions, the truth probably lies somewhere between the extremes. *Rhododendron occidentale* is genetically compatible with twelve of the fourteen East Coast species, but its isolated range prevents natural hybridization. Two East Coast species, *R. canadense* and *R. vaseyi*, are lumped together taxonomically but are genetically incompatible with each other and with all other American species. Wild hybrids have been verified between numerous species pairs, especially in the Deep South where they are so common. In addition to the following pairs, some hybrids have been identified that involve three and perhaps even four species.

> *Rhododendron alabamense* × *R. canescens*
> *Rhododendron alabamense* × *R. periclymenoides*
> *Rhododendron arborescens* × *R. calendulaceum*
> *Rhododendron arborescens* × *R. cumberlandense*
> *Rhododendron arborescens* × *R. periclymenoides*
> *Rhododendron arborescens* × *R. prinophyllum*
> *Rhododendron arborescens* × *R. viscosum*
> *Rhododendron atlanticum* × *R. periclymenoides*
> *Rhododendron calendulaceum* × *R. canescens*
> *Rhododendron calendulaceum* × *R. cumberlandense*
> *Rhododendron calendulaceum* × *R. periclymenoides*
> *Rhododendron calendulaceum* × *R. prinophyllum*
> *Rhododendron calendulaceum* × *R. viscosum*
> *Rhododendron canescens* × *R. atlanticum*
> *Rhododendron canescens* × *R. austrinum*
> *Rhododendron canescens* × *R. flammeum*
> *Rhododendron canescens* × *R. periclymenoides*
> *Rhododendron prinophyllum* × *R. periclymenoides*

Identifying hybrids in the field is relatively easy, especially between an orange or red species and a pink or white species. The resulting plants frequently have vivid pink flowers with yellow or orange blotches. Hybrids between two fragrant pink species or between two nonfragrant orange or red species can be very difficult to identify. If the diagnostic characteristics of an azalea such as bloom time, flower color, flower tube glands, and floral bud scale glands are close to type-form definition, identification is relatively easy. Identification is very difficult, however, in the many azaleas that appear to be species but whose family trees, if available, would reveal intermittent gene exchange with other species. Evidence of long-term gene exchange can be found in most East Coast species, especially in overlap areas between species with large distribution ranges. Like people, azaleas are very adept at concealing their ancestries.

Today we probably have more azalea species than in the past. Several authorities have theorized that the twelve species with five anthers could have speciated through hybridization from a red similar to *Rhododendron cumberlandense* and a white similar to *R. arborescens*. These changes were probably brought about over the millennia by forces of glaciation. Our present climate is thought to be a warm period between glacial advances. As the last advance began to recede some 16,000 years ago, the azaleas kept their distance but followed the glacial fronts northward and redistributed themselves through the basic seed dispersal mechanisms of wind —probably tornadoes—and water flow. These periodic disturbances, combined with wildfires, deforestation, and agricultural practices, undoubtedly presented hybridizing opportunities not seen in the species' ranges as they exist today.

In March of 1951, Henry T. Skinner embarked on a journey of epic proportions to study southern azaleas, and while his work was primarily descriptive in nature, his discoveries remain valid. Between March 18 and August 12, 1951, he and his cohorts traveled 25,000 miles by car inside a rectangle from Florida to Texas and from Missouri to coastal Virginia, crossing Alabama and Georgia several times. They made collections from 7360 plants, both species and hybrids, and traveled countless miles by foot. Using perforated cards, Skinner indexed data on flower color, flower blotch, plant growth habit, flower tube hairs, bud scale hairs, and leaf hairs. Perhaps his most important finding was that no species is stable across its range. This supports other studies and personal observations that suggest that hybridization is an ongoing process and that most species show evidence of past or recent gene infiltration from other species. There is hope on the horizon that better ways will be developed to analyze azaleas. Until then perhaps the best way to resolve the issue is to use a slight twist on an old adage: if it look like a duck, it's probably mostly duck.

Chapter 3

Collecting Azaleas

In late winter as the Earth revolves around the Sun toward the vernal equinox, a new seven-month azalea season begins in March in the Deep South of the United States. As the sun angle increases the various species bloom in a methodical progression northward and inland and upward in elevation along the Atlantic seaboard. The season ends in June in the New England states but lingers on into July at the higher elevations in the Appalachian Mountains. In an apparent reversal of the natural order of things, the season ends back in the South, very near where it began, in a small area along the Alabama-Georgia border. Here the last three species put on a final show of color in July, August, and well into September. On the West Coast the single species there (*Rhododendron occidentale*) begins its season in early May near the Pacific Ocean in northwestern Baja, Mexico, coastal California, and Oregon, and then moves inland to climb the western slopes of the Sierra Nevada well into August.

On the Road Again

As a new azalea season begins one of the best ways to beat the winter doldrums is to take an azalea trip. For several years Nick Anastos, Ewin Jenkins, and I have made several annual trips is search of azaleas, meanwhile keeping an eye out for any other unusual plants we might encounter. While some collecting is done, in truth these trips are really excuses to travel the rural back-roads of the South. In today's fast-paced world, there are few things that slow the apparent progression of time more than being in the woods. Georgia, North Carolina, and South Carolina, where most of our exploring is done, are similar in that each is composed of three distinct geographic zones. The sandy coastal plains border the Atlantic Ocean and are ancient seabeds. The rolling foothills of the piedmont stretch from the coastal plains to the mountains. The third area, and most diverse from a botanical standpoint, are the Appalachian Mountains.

Collecting azaleas does not require academic training, but it does help to be familiar with plants. Years ago an old plant collector was asked how he had been able to find so many unusual plants. His answer was short and to the point, "It's easy to spot a stranger." As he so simply put it, the key to finding something unusual is to know what a plant is supposed to look like. To make the point of not following this rule, another plant collector spotted a bright pink azalea with double flowers in a rural farmyard many miles from his home. He stopped and asked the owner if the plant was for sale and was told that it was not. He drove out of his way for several years to plead with the farmer, who finally agreed to sell it to him for an undisclosed amount. (We can guess that he didn't get if for a song.) Pleased with his find, the new owner sent a bag of flowers to a friend to determine if the plant was good enough to be propagated commercially. To the new owner's dismay, the azalea was identified as an old cultivated variety the farmer had probably bought at a local garden center. Undoubtedly, the farmer has enjoyed telling the story many times over, and the amount he was paid for it has surely grown with the passage of time.

Keeping the lesson learned by this collector in mind, we set out each year with renewed anticipation. Our collecting gear is simple: hand pruners, plastic bags for storing cuttings and layers, gelatin capsules for collecting pollen, and a small digger for removing roots and layers. Nick carries a small backpack, but Ewin insists on dragging along a GI duffel bag large enough to be slept in if the need arises. Through trial and error, I settled on a red-and-blue Scottish plaid bag made of woven plastic, similar to car upholstery material used in the 1950s. The key to being seen in the woods with a lady's shopping bag is to walk with a sense of purpose and avoid eye contact with strangers. So far it has worked.

As we drive from site to site, Nick and Ewin carry on long conversations about the medicinal and toxic qualities of plants. The discussions are interesting, but my frame of reference is that plants without bark and bright flowers are weeds. (I do admit, however, to giving some of the newer hostas a second glance.) Ewin is on a mission to find the world's best hotdog and is like a modern-day Don Quixote intent on skewering wieners instead of windmills. We don't know his criteria for evaluation, but South Carolina's best rank low on his scale. (A man of medicine should have some concerns about saturated fats, but he apparently missed that lecture.) Nick has the ability to cover large areas of ground and revive the cuttings and pieces of plants we bring back. The material is triaged in his shadehouse and emerges later ready to go in the ground.

In our earlier years of collecting, we found that going to a site known by someone was better than stumbling along blindly in unfamiliar territory. Many years ago Fred Galle told us of a plant collector in Georgia who was noted for his colorful collection of azaleas. Finding him was a relatively simple matter, as was getting an invitation to visit him. His plants were very colorful, and he gave us detailed directions to a nearby site where he had collected the plants, along with a warning that the residents of the area were very protective of them. The plants were easy enough to find and better than we had expected. While the temptation is always there to dig plants, there are several reasons to avoid this, one of which is the potential of an overnight stay in a local jail. Using our best collecting techniques, we took cuttings, collected pollen, and removed small layers. Some of those plants are still in our gardens today.

Avery's Garden

In the mid-1980s I heard that an old plant collector, who lived in a remote area in the mountains of a nearby state, had a large collection of azaleas but that he would not part with any of them. That admonition alone was enough to spark my "we'll-see" attitude. A few months later I took a chance and stopped by to see him. Avery and his wife, Ada, lived in a white clapboard cottage by a small trout stream. As I walked toward the house a young coonhound looked up at me with disinterest from his dusty bed under the porch. I knocked, and Avery came to the door. He wore bib overalls, a plaid shirt, and a worn, brown suit-coat. As they say in the area, he was square of jaw and blue of eye. He spoke with a heavy Elizabethan brogue, revealing his Scottish-Irish ancestry. I explained the purpose of my visit, and probably due to my slow drawl and interest in plants, I was immediately accepted as a friend.

It took visits over several years to see all the plants Avery had in his garden. He had spent most of his adult life digging, growing, and shipping rhododendrons and azaleas to the northeastern states, a practice that has since been discontinued. As the plants passed through his nursery, he had kept some of the more unusual ones and planted them around their home. On the first visit we walked around the grounds; he pointed to plants with his hand-carved walking stick and told the stories of how he had acquired them. Understanding Avery's pronunciation of azaleas and rhododendrons, a mixture of Latin and common names, was a challenge. He called *Rhododendron viscosum* "visty cosum." *Rhododendron nudiflorum* (*R. periclymenoides*) was corrupted to "nuji-flower." *Rhododendron calendulaceum* was close as "candy-lacey," ditto *R. arborescens* as "arborestus." But *R. roseum* (*R. prinophyllum*) remains a puzzle as "rosy-queenyestus." He referred to *Leucothoë fontanesiana* (fetter-bush) as "dog hobble," a perfectly good name for a plant whose viney limbs have strangled more than one good coonhound, and *Kalmia latifolia* (mountain laurel) was "ivy," as expected. *Rhododendron catawbiense* was "purple laurel," *R. maximum* was "white laurel," and *R. minus* was "punctatum."

At the end of the first visit I asked about his bright yellow *Rhododendron arborescens* and fragrant red *R. calendulaceum*, two of the unusual plants I had been told he had. He stalled by saying that they were probably around somewhere and that he would try to locate them when they bloomed the following year. Probably to keep my interest up, he gave me an azalea that he referred to as a "double nuji-flower." That sounded interesting, so I counted the trip a success. The following spring the nuji-flower displayed its doubleness by exposing pale pink flowers with gold blotches, obviously a *R. calendulaceum* × *R. periclymenoides* hybrid. To Avery "double" meant bicolored.

As good luck would have it, the next summer Avery called to let me know that the "flagrant" (fragrant) candy-lacey was in bloom and that I should come up to see it. The invitation was accepted. As bad luck would have it, we walked to a corner of the garden to find a large rooster pecking away at the last few flowers on the small plant. As suspected, the ragged flower tubes and leaves indicated the plant was a *R. arborescens* ×

R. cumberlandense hybrid, which also explained its fragrance. In a run of good luck, however, the bright yellow arborestus was in full bloom. It, too, appeared to be a hybrid of the same parentage, though it was not fragrant. Avery suggested I dig a part of it, which I did as quickly and casually as possible. Later in the day Avery wanted to take me to a nearby mountain to see a *R. maximum* with variegated foliage. In another run of bad luck, we found the roadside plant easily enough but a highway "beautification crew" had demolished the plant with a bush-hog a few days earlier. The yellow streaks in the drying foliage were still plainly visible. To avenge its assault the splintered stump never resprouted.

On another visit a year or so later, Avery wanted to show me a blue ivy at a friends house some distance away. I doubted that such a plant existed but a mountain laurel with blue flowers would surely put a smile on Dick Jaynes's face. Upon arriving, he disappeared in the friend's house for some time. When he reentered the car, smelling of fresh moonshine, he apologized and said his friend had decided not to let anyone see the plant. On the way back the thought came to mind that even though I was driving, Avery had just taken me for a ride to his afternoon drink. He never mentioned the blue ivy again.

In 2001, some ten years since the last visit, I was in the area and stopped by to check on Avery and Ada. The old hound was not in his customary spot under the porch. I walked up to the door, somewhat tentatively, gave the customary short knock afforded to friends and walked in. Avery sat by the small woodstove, his favorite spot, and began talking as if I had been there the day before. He explained that Ada was away visiting relatives, but she was doing fine. We took the customary walk around the grounds, a bit slower this time, and as we walked by the plant the rooster had attacked some years ago, he pointed to it with his cane and asked if I would like to take it with me. As I dug part of it, he rambled on about the plants he had seen over the year and lamented the fact that people nowadays seem to be too hurried to care much for them. At the end of the visit Avery waved good-bye with his cane as I drove away, perhaps for the last time. Though none of the plants in Avery's garden were spectacular, when they bloom here in South Carolina each spring they bring back fond memories of the visits with Avery and Ada.

Mother Nature

Several years ago we had finished our collecting for the day on an over-grown bald in the Appalachians. On the way down, clouds suddenly moved in accompanied by an immediate drop in temperature of perhaps 20 degrees. This was a classic example of a microburst, a cold, palpable downdraft of dense air that can put an airplane into free-fall in an instant. Without warning it began to hail in torrents. The hail soon filled the steep, rutted trail, making walking all but impossible. It stripped leaves and small limbs from the trees as we slid down the slope to the gap where we were parked. We hastily threw our gear in the trunk and drove slowly down the mountain, soaked and painfully bruised from the hail, which had covered the road to a depth of three inches in less than ten minutes. One of our cars still carries scars from that incident.

Not satisfied, we returned the next year to try again. The top of the mountain is densely wooded and covered with granite boulders and ferns almost waist high. With no trails to follow, walking was difficult. On this trip we stumbled onto a copperhead snake that quickly damp-ened our zest. After we gave the azaleas a quick once-over, we left to try another area. The following year we decided to give the mountain one last try, and this time Nick stumbled onto a large timber rattlesnake in the same area we had seen the copperhead the year before. There may be good azaleas on that mountain, but the three-strike rule is good enough for me.

Lost and Found

A few years ago I took what would become an ill-advised solo trip to a spur off the Appalachian Trail. After the long hike to the 5000-foot sum-mit and before any collecting could be done, a slow-moving wall of dense clouds crept through the trees. As they closed in, the woods grew silent and the mood changed from cheerful to dark and foreboding. With rain likely to follow I started back to the trail, but I quickly realized the dead trees I had used as landmarks on the way in were no longer visible. Sim-ply put, I became lost without taking a step. Going downhill would lead to a stream and it to a small house some five miles away. By staying calm,

I reasoned, getting out by sundown should be no problem. Taking a deep breath I set off in what seemed to be the right direction. After stumbling along slowly for five minutes or so I came to a dim game trail and turned onto it. In a short distance it came to a dead end. Turning around I backtracked and soon came to the main trail. As I gathered my wits I realized I had never been more than a few hundred yards away from the main trail. Looking around to see that no one was watching—slim chance of that— I bravely hitched up my backpack and headed down the mountain as if nothing had happened.

On the way down the rain began. As luck would have it this stretch of trail has a low, log shelter for hikers, which I ducked into. On a nail in the wall hung a notebook filled with notes written by overnight hikers. One passage was particularly interesting. A college student proudly recounted the ten miles she had hiked on her first day on the trail. She had seen colorful flowers, presumably azaleas, but complained that the trail was so rough that she had gotten jockey itch (her words) in spite of her best efforts. She closed by wishing she were home on her mom's couch under a warm quilt. Smart girl.

As the sound of the rain and the buzz of mosquitoes increased I decided to head toward the car, a long mile away. Surely someone who had so skillfully navigated himself out of the wilderness without the aid of a compass could survive a downpour. The steep trail was slick but easy to see. As I slogged along, cold, wet, and tired, I wondered how long it would take for this trip to become a fond memory. As of now, there is still no humor in it.

Found and Lost

On a return trip from the Snowbird Mountains in North Carolina some years ago, Nick and I spotted an eastern hemlock (*Tsuga canadensis*) with a large variegated limb in a farmyard near the road. The stark green and white pattern looked a bit unusual, but there it was nonetheless. On the way home I imagined fields of this plant, a species that is easy to propagate, carefully pruned and growing in long rows. This would become the world's first preflocked Christmas tree and would become the standard for the holidays. 'Snowflakes' would be a perfect name.

Months later I was in the area and stopped by to take a closer look and found that the snowflakes were gone. As I puzzled over the situation, a white splash appeared out of nowhere, so I thought, and landed on the limb. Peering up I spotted a lone pigeon in a tall oak over the smaller hemlock. Just then several more pigeons flew out of a nearby barn and joined their friend. As if on cue, more snowflakes fell and the limb began to return to its original splendor. As I pulled away the disappointment soon gave way to amusement. The memory and humor of the situation are far more important than any value the tree may have had. Looking back, there are probably several morals to this story.

Roadside Treasure

During the 2002 American Rhododendron Society/Azalea Society of America joint convention in Atlanta, Ewin Jenkins and his wife, Janet, were on a tour that stopped by the house of Ferrol Sams, a physician and novelist, and his wife, Helen Sams, a physician. While walking through the garden, Ewin spotted an exceptionally bright rose azalea in full bloom, obviously of hybrid origin. He took some photographs, and a few weeks later we examined them and decided that it might be a candidate for the azaleas we were selecting for propagation. We had met Ferrol a few years earlier, so we gave him a call about the azalea. In his inimitable, molasses-smooth drawl Ferrol explained how they had acquired it. A few years earlier on a trip from their northern Georgia cabin, Helen spotted it growing along the roadside. They turned the car around to give it a closer look and were so taken by its bright color that they removed all the flowers to hide it from view. Ferrol explained with a chuckle that there are actually scoundrels around who will steal plants, so they decided to denude it to keep it from falling into the wrong hands. Later that year they returned to the site and dug a part of the plant, which they took to their cabin. In later trips, they stopped by the scene of the crime and dug several of the smaller plants that had sprouted from the roots left behind. They now have several large plants from the original, which is probably still growing by the roadside, that is, if some scoundrel hasn't stolen it.

Chapter 4

Growing Azaleas

As colorful as azaleas are, they have never been common garden plants. Some of the reasons for this are that they are not commercially available in many areas, they are not well known to the public, and they have an undeserved reputation of being difficult to grow. Azaleas have a few cultural requirements that must be met, but doing so is not very complicated. Armed with a little knowledge the average gardener can grow them successfully. As more colorful and vigorous selections become available, their popularity will almost certainly increase.

Selecting Azaleas

Because each azalea cultivar (cultivated variety) has a unique genetic makeup, some understanding of how to choose one for a specific site and climate can be helpful. Although most azaleas purchased from garden centers have tags listing parentage and preferred growing conditions, this is not always the case. If not, some garden centers will have a specialist on hand who can give assistance. Azaleas bought from mail-order sources will usually have this information in the catalog, and it should be given due consideration. An up-to-date cultivar list can also be of assistance in making good choices for various garden conditions and climates. Even if all the planting, fertilizing, and watering requirements are met, however, an azalea developed from hardy, high-elevation species may not thrive in a warm, low-elevation situation.

When purchasing an azalea, the color if its flowers and time of bloom should be taken into account. Red flowers do not show up well against brown or red brick walls, and azaleas that bloom late in the summer may suffer if planted in open, exposed areas. Azaleas that live naturally near watercourses may not like hot, dry sites, and azaleas from the Deep South may not be hardy in the colder areas of the Northeast. These and other factors will become more evident as the gardener becomes familiar with the nuances of growing the many available azalea cultivars.

Color Stability

When purchasing an azalea the owner has a right to expect the color of the flowers to be as described on the label, but there are several reasons why this may not be true. In order for azaleas to be a marketable product, they have to be subjected to the fast-growth methods used in commercial nurseries. This usually consists of daily watering, a constant dilute drip of acid fertilizer, confinement to black plastic containers sitting on black weed-control fabric, and a covering of woven, black shade-cloth. Watering moderates the excessive heat generated by the plastic and keeps them in an active state of growth. This culture is foreign to azaleas in the wild but allows nursery plants to be pushed along several years in one growing season. Having endured these extreme but necessary growing conditions, an azalea that has bright red flowers may temporarily have orange or even yellow flowers, and a pink selection may have white flowers. If the loss of color is due to nursery conditions, the flowers should regain their color in a year or so in a typical garden situation.

A second problem is that some azaleas are given catchy names the plants may never live up to. For example a cultivar described as vivid yellow may in fact be light yellow. This is a result of our tendency to make things sound more attractive than they are. Another factor that influences the color of azaleas is sunlight. Some azaleas have brighter flowers in exposed situations than in shady areas, and low night temperatures may also intensify flower color. Another consideration is that many azaleas, especially hybrids, go through color changes, with some becoming darker and some becoming lighter as they age. Finally, and probably for a variety of reasons, azaleas seem to have lighter flowers some years than others.

Soil Acidity and Fertilizer

Two of the most discussed and confusing issues in growing azaleas are those of soil pH and fertilizer. These factors are closely tied together and are very complex at the atomic and molecular levels. For those of us who are not interested in delving into the mysterious aspects of soil chemistry, we need to know only a few basics to be successful at growing azaleas.

A good starting point is to have the soil tested by a county agent in areas where azaleas are to be planted. Another source of information about soil fertility is to inquire at a local fertilizer supplier or garden center. Soil pH (potential Hydrogen) is measured on a scale from 0 to 14, with 7 being neutral. Soils with a pH below 7 are said to be acidic and alkaline if above 7. Azaleas grow best in acidic soils from 4.5 to 6.5, with 5.0 to 6.0 being ideal. Few gardens have soils that are too acidic, but if the pH is too high it can be decreased by amending the top 6 inches of soil with organic matter and the appropriate amounts of ferrous sulfate or sulfur.

Fertilizing is another issue that is frequently made more complicated than it needs to be for the average gardener. Of the nine macronutrients that are necessary for plant growth, azaleas extract carbon, hydrogen, and oxygen from the air and water. Additionally they require varying amounts of calcium, magnesium, nitrogen, phosphorus, potassium, and sulfur. Seven micronutrients—boron, chlorine, copper, iron, manganese, molybdenum, and zinc—are required in smaller amounts.

Fertilizers are labeled as to the amount of nitrogen (N), phosphorus (P), and potassium (K) they contain. One labeled 15–10–9 has 15 percent nitrogen, 10 percent phosphorus, and 9 percent potassium by weight. Gardeners should purchase fertilizers specially formulated for rhododendrons, azaleas, and evergreens. Although they are more expensive, they differ from fast-release 10–10–10 agricultural fertilizers by releasing their nutrients over a longer period of time and containing the necessary micronutrients needed for good azalea health. By following this list of simple rules, azaleas should do well in most garden situations:

Purchase a slow-release granular or resin-coated fertilizer, with micronutrients, that is formulated for azaleas and rhododendrons.
Avoid the use of inexpensive, fast-release agricultural fertilizers.

Fertilize a newly planted containerized azalea little, if any, the
first year because residual fertilizer in the plant will carry it
until the next spring.

After new growth appears in the spring of the second year, add
no more than ⅛ cup of fertilizer to an azalea less than 2
feet tall and no more than ¼ cup of fertilizer to an azalea
more than 2 feet tall. Taller established azaleas can take up
to ½ cup every other year or so, provided it is scattered
evenly around the drip-line of the plant.

Do not fertilize azaleas in late summer or autumn, because
current growth needs to harden off before going into the
winter months.

Keep azaleas lightly mulched at all times.

If an azalea looks happy, leave it alone.

An imbalance between soil pH and the availability of iron can cause
a reduction in chlorophyll in azalea leaves, resulting in a condition known
as iron chlorosis. This problem is characterized by yellow leaves with green
veins and is frequently mistaken as a disease. Other factors can cause yellow leaves, but if the culprit is chlorosis, spray the foliage for a few days
with iron sulfate at a mixture of 1 ounce per 2 gallons of water. If this fails
and the yellow leaves later develop reddish purple blotches and brown
tips and margins, this is probably an indication of a magnesium defi-
ciency. For this condition, spray the foliage with magnesium sulfate
(epsom salts) at a mixture of 1 ounce per 2 gallons of water.

Planting

One of the best ways to understand and duplicate the soil conditions preferred by azaleas is to visit a site where they grow naturally. Azaleas can
be found in a variety of locations, from damp stream margins to dry, rocky
hillsides to high, windswept mountaintops. If an azalea could be removed
intact from the ground, as much as a third of its total mass would be in
the form of roots. Due to the need for adequate oxygen and moisture,
roots spread out radially from the plant in the porous top layer of soil
and just below a layer of decomposing leaves.

When they are in an active state of growth, roots follow their noses outward, diving deeper in the ground during dry periods and moving closer to the surface during wet periods. They have the ability to grow through, around, under, or over any obstacles they encounter, giving the roots a zigzag growth pattern.

In an effort to help a containerized azalea regrow roots in a radial pattern, the first step is to remove it from the container and take a close look at the root-ball. Ideally, small, fibrous roots will have grown down the sides of the pot and across the bottom. If an azalea is left in a pot too long, however, the roots will grow into a solid mass, creating a condition referred to as "root-bound" or "pot-bound." In either case the azalea should not go directly from the container to a permanent site.

The second step is to cut off the bottom one-third of the root-ball with a sharp knife. The root-ball should also be cut from top to bottom in two or three areas. While this damages the roots, it is the best way to insure the survival of the plant. After making the vertical cuts, hold the root-ball in an upright position and tear the ends of the roots outward from the bottom (Figure 6A). With some work the roots can be splayed apart in a relatively flat position, much like they grow naturally. Some soil will be lost from the root-ball during this process, which is actually beneficial to promoting regeneration of new roots. Some nurseries sell field-grown azaleas that, in many instances, can more easily make the transition to permanent beds. Again, the root-ball should be examined and excess soil should be removed with a trowel to expose the cut ends of the roots.

The final, equally important step is the preparation of the bed for the azalea. If a root-ball is 8 inches wide, dig a hole a minimum of 16 inches wide and 12 inches deep and set the soil aside. The soil will be sand, loam, or clay, and each will benefit from the addition of organic matter. Finely ground pine bark, usually referred to as soil conditioner, or composted leaf mold will help the soil hold moisture and provide additional air pockets. Amend the soil removed from the hole in a 1:1 ratio with the organic matter and fill the hole half full. Place the azalea on the amended soil, with the top of the root-ball sitting about 1 inch above ground level. While watering with a garden hose, slowly backfill the hole with the remaining amended soil, making sure the cut ends of the roots make contact with the soil.

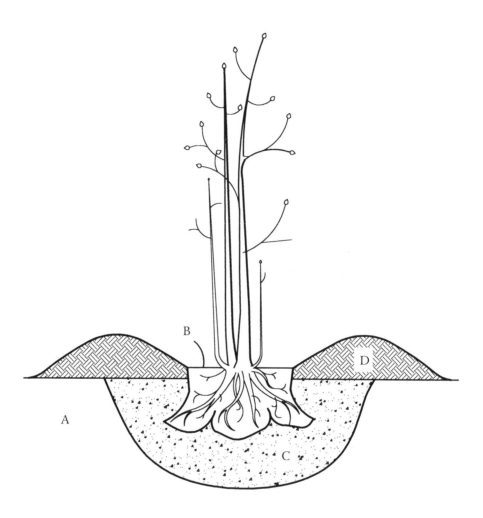

Figure 6. Properly planting an azalea in undisturbed soil (A) requires lacerating the root-ball (B), amending the soil (C), and mulching (D). Drawing by Allen Cantrell

Because the names of azaleas may be forgotten in time, it is a good idea to label them. This also allows visitors to check their names without having to ask. As simple as labels sound, numerous articles have been written in journals on how to tag azaleas after they are planted. Aluminum tags, which can be embossed with a dull pencil, are commonly used. To avoid the possibility of damage to the tagged limb, which is reported to be a common occurrence, the bare aluminum wire should be replaced with plastic coated wire. Thick plastic labels that can be written on with a permanent marker are also available. These pointed labels work best when pushed into the mulch to prevent damage from ultraviolet rays. Leave the blunt ends showing above the mulch so the labels can be located easily.

Mulching

Mulching is an easy process but very important to the health of an azalea. It also has weed-control benefits and generally improves the appearance of a planting. As found in the woods the area around an azalea is usually covered with a layer of decomposing leaves, twigs, and limbs. This layer keeps the roots cool during the summer and warm during the winter, and it provides a constant low-level source of nutrients. Duplicate this by loosely covering the area around the azalea to a depth of 2 to 3 inches with leaf mold, ground pine bark, pine straw, or aged wood chips. As these materials decompose additional applications may be needed. Arrange the mulch in a ring around the plant to allow it to act as dam to hold moisture during watering until the roots become established in the surrounding soil. Avoid freshly ground wood chips because they will deplete the plant of nitrogen during decomposition.

Watering

An experienced gardener can remove an azalea from a pot, tear the roots apart, dig a hole, plant the azalea, kick a few leaves over the hole, and throw on a handful of fertilizer in less than five minutes. If it is not watered properly the first year, however, the azalea will die just as surely as if planted by an amateur who takes two hours to do the same job. When a containerized root-ball is torn apart and properly planted, the roots will start to regenerate in a few days. Until these new roots fully integrate themselves into the soil of their new home—a process that can take several weeks—the plant will lose water rapidly through normal leaf transpiration. The soil around a newly planted azalea may be saturated but the root-ball itself may be bone dry. During hot, windy weather an azalea can dehydrate to the point of death in a few days. This problem can be solved in several ways.

Hand watering with a plastic pail every three or four days is a simple fix for a few azaleas close to a source of water. If located further away, a garden hose, with nozzle removed, can be adjusted to a slow drip for a few hours. For larger plantings a temporary sprinkling system may have to be installed. If these steps are followed through the first summer, little supplemental watering will be required in subsequent years.

Pruning

Azaleas need very little pruning and do not like to be trimmed into reindeer or given flat-topped haircuts. Remove dead limbs back to live wood and trim vigorous suckers back to the base of the plant. Limbs may occasionally grow out of bounds and should be cut back to the general outline of the plant. As azaleas age some will outgrow their location and may need to be pruned heavily. A healthy azalea can be cut back to ground level with no ill effects. This is best done in the spring, when the plant is in a state of active growth. Enjoy the flowers and then cut the plant back to 2 inches above ground level with lopping shears or a chainsaw. In a few days tiny red buds will appear just below the cuts and will quickly elongate into vigorous shoots in a matter of weeks. With some luck these shoots may set flower buds for the next year, but in most instances this will take place the following year.

Removing old flower trusses, referred to as deadheading, is an annual event for some gardeners. The argument is that it makes the plants look neat and improves bud set for the next year. Both of these reasons are probably true, but as plants get taller this becomes impractical. Because there is no evidence that deadheading damages plants and the impulse to have clean plants may be overwhelming, deadhead away and enjoy the exercise.

Vigorous, tall-growing azalea species and hybrids, especially older ones, can be pruned into small trees. Select and remove all but the three largest trunks at ground level and limb-up the trunks to a height of about 6 feet. If the lower trunks are pruned of new growth as it appears, the top of the plant will broaden and take on a treelike shape. This approach is best used on plants that are in exposed areas.

Transplanting

Occasionally the amount of shade above an established azalea may increase, causing it to slow or stop flower production. A good fix for this is to give it a new home. Moving an old azalea that was originally purchased in a container to a new site is easy to do because the roots will be not be as widely spread as on a wild plant. The move can be made at any time of year. Dig a circle outside the root-ball with a sharp spade, trying to keep the soil intact with the roots. Pry the root-ball out of the ground and move to the new site. Place in its new bed, which should be wider than the root-ball, and backfill with good soil. Mulch, water thoroughly, and fertilize with a pail of dilute liquid fertilizer. Water frequently until the severed roots have regenerated and grown into the soil of the new bed.

The issue of transplanting azaleas from the wild is frowned on by some, but in recent years organized plant rescues have preserved many plants that otherwise would have been lost to urban sprawl. For those who dig wild plants, for whatever reason, following a few simple rules can help to insure that they will live to bloom again. The best time to move an azalea is while it is in bloom and in an active state of growth. As harsh as it may sound, the plant should be cut back to near ground level, making sure all small limbs and leaves are removed. Use a sharp spade to cut the roots in a circle around the trunks out to a width of not more than 12 inches on either side of the plant. Pry up the root-ball, and remove all soil. Place the naked, mutilated plant in a large plastic bag and plant in a temporary bed in a day or so.

One azalea rescuer rakes an area down to bare soil under tall pines and puts the bare rootstocks on top of the ground in rows. The roots are covered with rotted sawdust to a depth of about 10 inches and the sawdust is then compacted to a depth of about 6 inches by walking on it. Finally, the entire area is mulched with 3 inches of loose pine straw. In a few weeks the cut-back trunks will begin to show new growth and will sometimes set a few buds for the next year. The azaleas should stay in the sawdust bed for a year or so before being transplanted to a permanent location. To lessen concerns about moving rescued azaleas, it should be noted that the cut ends of the roots left in the ground always sprout new growth in a few weeks. In time these sprouts will form a ring of plants to replace the one that was dug.

Azalea Pests and Diseases

If azaleas can escape the damage inflicted by lawnmowers, string trimmers, and deer, they have a good chance of living long and healthy lives. While they are not entirely free of ailments, azaleas do not require excessive health care. A few insect pests and fungi, however, can cause problems, and the following list includes some of the ones more commonly encountered. Once the culprit is diagnosed, most can be controlled with one or more applications of the appropriate insecticide or fungicide.

INSECT PESTS

Azalea bud larva, *Orthosia hibisci.*—The larva of a fruitworm moth has become a fairly common pest in recent years in the Southeast. The moth lays an egg in a flower bud. The resulting larva eats the immature flowers inside and finally chews its way out of the bud. If a flower bud fails to open, look for a small hole in the side of the bud. Once the telltale holes appear, most of the damage has been done. To prevent infestation, spraying with an appropriate insecticide should be done in early spring several weeks prior to bloom time.

Azalea bark scale, *Eriocossus azaleae.*—Azalea bark scales are small insects that attach themselves to bark, frequently near the base of a plant. They conceal themselves under soft waxy gray or white egg sacs that are difficult to destroy with insecticides. After the eggs hatch the immature larvae attach themselves to nearby bark to mature and repeat the cycle, and they are susceptible to insecticides at this time. A small number of scales can be rubbed away by hand, but infestations can deform large areas of bark and may cause entire limbs to die.

Azalea caterpillar, *Datana major.*—Caterpillars of several species of moths chew on azalea leaves, with the most common species being *Datana major.* The caterpillars raise their heads and tails in unison when disturbed. Small limbs containing caterpillars can be broken off and destroyed, and larger infestations should be eradicated with pesticides.

Azalea whitefly, *Pealius azalea.*—Azalea whitefly is tiny moth that penetrates and feeds on the sap of azalea leaves, as do their larvae, making the leaves damaged and discolored. Heavy infestations can completely defoliate plants in closed propagation areas and can be very difficult to control.

Black vine weevil, *Otiorhynchus sulcatus.*—Black vine weevils are ⅜-inch long beetles with snouts that can cause substantial damage to azaleas. Mature weevils chew leaf margins in a characteristic notched pattern, but the hidden larvae eat roots and girdle larges stems at or below ground level, causing the death of stems or entire small plants.

Lacebug, *Staphinitis pyriodes.*—Azalea lacebug is a common pest of azaleas grown in full sun. The tiny insects have delicate, lacelike wing patterns and are erroneously referred to as "lacewing flies." The undersides of damaged leaves show tell-tale holes where the bugs have sucked the sap away, as well as small black tarlike spots of excrement and spent larval casts. Spraying should be restricted to the undersides of leaves.

Leaf miner, *Caloptilia azaleella.*—Leaf-miners, also known as leaf-rollers, are the larvae of tiny moths. The moths tie the edges of unfolding leaves together and lay eggs inside the leaf tubes. As the larvae increase in size, damage to leaves increases. As the season progresses, the larvae mature into adults and the sequence is repeated, resulting in damage to new leaves that unfold later in the season.

Southern red mite, *Oligonychus ilicis.*—Several species of spider mites can damage azaleas, especially the southern red mite. Spider mites have eight legs, a one-piece body, and are closely related to ticks and spiders. They damage azalea leaves by penetrating and sucking sap from leaf cells, which kills large areas of leaves. Affected leaves become bronzed, bleached, yellow, or gray and finally drop. Eggshells and skin casts can be found on the undersides of leaves.

Stem borer, *Obera myops.*—Longhorn beetles feed on the midveins of azalea leaves, causing them to curl downward. The slender beetles girdle new shoots twice, up to 1 inch apart, and deposit an egg between the girdles, causing the tip to wilt and die. When the larva hatches, it tunnels down the stem toward the roots, forming holes along the way from which to expel its sawdustlike frass. The journey to the root-ball can take two years. Cut away damaged stems or pump insecticide into the hole to kill the larva.

FUNGAL DISEASES

Leaf gall, *Exobasidium vaccinii.*—Azalea leaf galls, which can also affect flowers and buds, are swollen masses filled with an astringent liquid that make their presence known more in periods of cool, wet weather. Usually the galls are covered with a light gray powder. After a time the fleshy galls shrivel into small, hard lumps. Destroy them by hand picking.

Leaf rust, *Puccinniastrum myrtilii.*—Leaves damaged by rust first exhibit circular chlorotic spots on their upper surfaces, followed by yellow or orange sootlike spores underneath. The symptoms appear in late summer and fall and can cause plants to completely defoliate. Plants usually survive but may be susceptible to other diseases and cold weather stresses.

Petal blight, *Ovulina azaleae.*—Petal blight is more common in damp weather and appears as brown spots on flowers. The brown spots soon spread and entire flowers become disfigured and turn to slimy masses.

Powdery mildew, *Microspharea penicillate.*—This infection appears as a white to light gray powder on both surfaces of leaves. It is more common in areas with poor air drainage or in damp shade. Some azalea cutivars are more susceptible than others.

Root rot, *Phytophthera cinnamomi.*—This is the most problematic disease of azaleas, especially if caused by *Phytophthera cinnamomi.* As infected root systems die, plants appear wilted. Root rot is common in azaleas planted too deep or in wet sites with poor drainage. Replace diseased plants with healthy ones and ensure good drainage.

Chapter 5

Landscaping with Azaleas

Landscaping with azaleas and companion plants requires some initial planning, but the process from start to finish can be a rewarding experience. A successful design can be as tranquil and serene as a formal Japanese garden or as relaxed and colorful as an English cottage garden. When a gardener decides to grow azaleas, one of three sites may be encountered. The first and most labor-intensive is a vacant woodlot. The second and more of a planning challenge is a small suburban backyard, sometimes totally devoid of trees. The third is a mature landscaped yard that lacks azaleas. There are no hard-and-fast rules to follow in any of these situations, but some suggestions may be of value.

Vacant Woodlot

Developing a woodlot into a functional azalea garden takes considerable work, but the finished product can substantially increase the value of the property. Once the decision has been made to develop a garden, the first obstacle to overcome may be the realization that well over half of the trees may have to be removed to provide enough sunlight for azaleas to bloom adequately. If the woodlot contains deciduous broadleaf trees, the first step in determining how many will have to be removed involves evaluating the amount of shade in the woodlot after the leaves have emerged in the spring. There will be a choice of removing all the smaller trees and leaving a few older, larger trees, or removing all the larger trees and leaving a greater number of younger trees. If the smaller trees are crowded, they will have developed narrow trunks with small lower limbs and will present fewer problems in the future as they continue to grow and their shade increases. Keep in mind that deciduous trees continue to grow in height and limb-spread over the years. All undesirable underbrush should be cleared, and trees should be thinned to 20 feet apart or more, which will give the area an open, parklike appearance.

A conifer woodlot, very common in some areas, will usually consist of tall trees with small tops. As many as half of these trees may have to be moved, as well as the dead stumps of lower limbs and leaning trees. Compared to deciduous trees, conifers provide less shade, the trees are usually smaller in diameter, and the amount of shade they provide will increase only slightly over the years. Trees in a conifer woodlot should be thinned to at least 10 feet apart. When finished, this type of woodlot will have a much different ambience than a deciduous woodlot. The needles on the trees and the ground are nonreflective and soften the glare that is typically reflected from deciduous leaves. Needles also have a habit of attaching themselves to the limbs of the azaleas below, so the gardener who wants the area to have a neat, clean appearance needs to take this into consideration. There is no practical way to remove the needles so the best approach is to learn to appreciate them as added decoration, along with the cones that will inevitably be there in large numbers.

An option to selectively thinning a woodlot to increase sunlight is to clear a large area in the center. Ideally, all trees in the area should be removed. The resulting arena can then be planted in grass or left natural. Azaleas and companion plants should be located around the perimeter, with the smaller perennials being located in front and the taller shrubs behind. A central structure—perhaps a gazebo or benches and statuary—can give the area a refined focal point. A path, preferably curved, should lead from the woodlot edge to the clearing and can be lined with plants of choice.

Once the trees to be removed are chosen, consider contracting with a tree removal service to do the work. Contracting to have the limbs and stumps removed, below ground level, with heavy-duty chippers and grinders should also be considered. The equipment will make quick work of the debris, leaving behind a large quantity of ground wood, bark, and soil that can be used elsewhere in the garden.

Once the woodlot is cleared, a path encircling the area should be laid out with plastic tape. After the debris is removed, the owner has the option of clearing the path down to bare soil or covering it with the remains of the ground stumps. Existing structures, such as large roots, rocks, gullies, and streams should be incorporated into the path and overall garden design.

Landscape timbers, sections of tree trunks, and rocks are frequently used to line woodlot paths. One of the problems with small landscape timbers is that they usually twist and warp with time, giving them an untidy appearance. Crossties warp very little but are too large and long for most sites. Small logs cut into 18-inch sections make good path liners, and their short length can more easily follow the curves of the path. In time they will rot, making good homes for ferns, mosses, and perennials.

New Yard

In suburban areas where the trend is to crowd homes onto small plots of land, growing azaleas may be more of a challenge. With some planning, however, even small backyards can be landscaped with azaleas. What these sites lack will probably be shade and rich soil. By making a sketch of the yard, a house oriented in any direction, with some modifications, can be adapted to grow azaleas (Figure 7).

By adding raised berms the yard can easily be given structure to eliminate large unbroken areas of grass, provide a rich growing medium for trees and shrubs, and provide microclimates in which to grow a wide range of perennials. Rich topsoil is the material of choice, but pine bark works well and is lighter and easier to work with. Pine bark comes in a wide range of grinds. After removal from pulp trees, the bark is ground, screened for size, and bagged or sold in bulk. The finest grind, about the consistency of sawdust, is usually sold as soil conditioner. The best grade for a berm has the consistency of cornflakes, but will have a considerable amount of fines (very small particles) mixed with it.

If there are existing trees in the yard with invasive root systems, such as yellow poplar (*Liriodendron tulipifera*) or American beech (*Fagus grandifolia*), consideration should be given to installing heavy-duty nonwoven polyethylene fabric over the areas where the berms will be placed. This

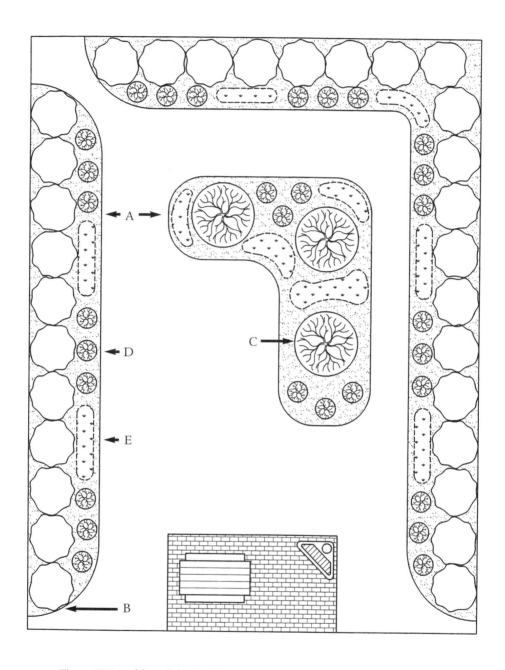

Figure 7. By adding (A) raised berms, (B) evergreen hedges, (C) small shade trees, (D) azaleas and shrubs, and (E) perennials, a typical backyard can be turned into a low-maintenance garden. Drawing by Allen Cantrell

type of fabric is durable yet allows water to seep through and will prevent roots from invading the damp berms.

The topsoil or ground bark should be spread in the designated areas to a depth of about 12 inches. Shaping the beds will be made much easier by the use of a small skid-steer tractor with rubber tires. Any existing trees should be incorporated into the design if possible. After the berms are completed, screening plants, small shade trees, azaleas, and shrubs should be planted according to the design. Purchase plants as large as can be afforded. As a final step, perennials should be added after the installation of the mulch. If the yard is planted with a creeping grass such as coastal Bermuda (*Cynodon dactylon*), the berms can be edged with safe and inconspicuous roll-top plastic borders to prevent grass from invading the beds. Clumping grasses such as fescue (*Festuca* spp.) and bluegrass (*Poa* spp.) are not invasive.

There are numerous mulches that can be used to finish the areas after the plants are installed. Ground and composted hardwood bark is shreddy and holds together better than pink bark. Pine straw works much the same and has a clean appearance when finished. Wood chips come in a variety of grinds, and some are dyed to give additional colors. Most dyed chips look unnatural, however, and should be avoided. If wood chips are used as mulch, they should be thoroughly aged and silvery in color when dry. A variety of crushed stones, lava rocks, and bricks are available as mulches, but they are expensive and will find their way into the grass in time, creating lawn-care problems.

Today's garden centers have many innovative cementitious landscaping materials, such as stepping-stones, pavers, retaining wall blocks, and crushed mulch. Although these materials can add to a landscape, if overused they can be distracting, so use the "less-is-best" philosophy and proceed with caution. These porous materials come in a wide range of neutral and not-so-neutral colors. If less offensive colors are desired, most can be dyed with one part exterior latex stain and two parts water. The diluted stain should be applied with a 2-gallon pump sprayer, such as used to apply herbicides or fertilizer. If stepping-stones are used in the yard design, they should be installed at ground level for safety reasons and in an asymmetrical pattern for aesthetic reasons. Grass will eventually creep onto them, which will soften their hard edges.

Existing Yard

An older yard, perhaps well landscaped in its day, can be given a new look by incorporating azaleas and new companion plants into the existing design. Because most azaleas prefer morning sun and afternoon shade, the first step is to find the areas most hospitable to azaleas. Along the shady sides of the house, examine the foundation shrubs and tag those to be removed or relocated. Removing a few shrubs scattered around the yard and along property lines should also be considered. When the design is finished, the shrubs to be removed can be dug by hand, an often tiring and frustrating task. An easier fix it to cut the shrubs back to just below ground level with lopping shears and leave the root-balls in the ground. Spray the cut ends of the trunks with an herbicide, and if new growth develops later, a final shot or two with the sprayer should finish them off for good. It should now be fairly easy to dig new holes between the cutbacks, planting the azaleas as described in chapter 4.

Companion Plants

An azalea garden needs a variety of companion plants for visual contrast and more gardeners are choosing to use native American plants. One of the reasons for this is that plants that grow in the same ranges with azaleas are usually easy to grow. Because many companion plants available to us are of European and Asian origin, the gardener who chooses this route will lose out on many fine selections, but the pursuit of suitable local species can add another interesting dimension to landscaping.

Companion plants for azaleas can be placed into five broad categories: groundcovers and edging plants, shrubs, small shade trees, evergreen screening trees, and screening vines. Plants selected for a semishady woodland garden will differ in some respects from those selected for open backyard gardens or foundation plantings. The followings lists contain a sampling of plants, many of which can be purchased on the Internet. Mature size, cold hardiness zone (see Appendix D), and heat tolerance should be primary considerations when selecting these plants. Most plants obtained from garden centers will have growing tips; most mail-order sources provide growing information in their catalogs.

GROUNDCOVERS AND EDGING PLANTS

Allegheny spurge, *Pachysandra procumbens.*—Allegheny spurge is found in the Appalachian Mountains but is adaptable to a much wider areas. It is a choice woodland creeper with mottled evergreen to semi-evergreen leaves and short spikes of small white to pink flowers in the spring. It spreads slowly to form a low bed, usually less than 8 inches tall. Zones 5–7.

Bearberry, *Arctostaphylos uva-ursi.*—Bearberry is an excellent groundcover that forms large mats with small white flowers followed by bright red fruit. The evergreen leaves are dark green and glossy. 'Massachusetts' is a vigorous cultivar with dark green leaves, and 'Vancouver Jade' has shiny green leaves. Zones 4–7.

Bleeding heart, *Dicentra eximia.*—Bleeding hearts have feathery, fernlike foliage and unusual heart-shaped white and rose flowers. They do best in well-drained soil. Cultivars include white 'Alba', and 'Boothman' has burgundy blue foliage and pink flowers. Similar *D. formosa* is more heat tolerant. Cultivars include white 'Aurora' and cherry-pink 'Luxuriant'. *Dicentra canadensis* (squirrel corn) and *D. culcullaria* (Dutchman's breeches) have white flowers and similar fernlike foliage. Zones 3–9.

Bloodroot, *Sanguinaria canadensis.*—Named because of its red sap, bloodroot is a member of the poppy family and has daisylike white flowers. The small plants have fleshy tubers and rounded blue-green leaves. They prefer damp, fertile soil. Zones 3–8.

Bog rosemary, *Andromeda polifolia.*—Bog rosemary, also known as andromeda, is a choice plant for the mountains of the South and gardens of the Northeast. It forms 18-inch-tall clumps that can spread to 3 feet in width in cool, moist soil. The leaves are narrow and dark green, and the urn-shaped flowers are light pink. 'Blue Ice' is a new selection with bright pink flowers and powdery blue foliage. Zones 3–6.

Christmas fern, *Polystichum acrostichoides.*—The evergreen Christmas fern is but one of a multitude of fern species and cultivars, deciduous and evergreen, available to gardeners. Most are easy to grow and tend to be long-lived. Fronds can be uncut, once-cut, twice-cut, or thrice-cut. Zones 4–9.

Cliffgreen, *Paxistima canbyi.*—Cliffgreen is a seldom-seen evergreen shrub that has several common names including rat-stripper and mountain-lover. The 1-foot mounding plants have small brownish red flowers and tiny evergreen leaves with notched margins. Leaves are greenish mahogany in the winter. Zones 4–8.

Coral bells, *Heuchera sanguinea.*—Breeding work with heucheras is making them a close second with Asiatic hostas as top-choice perennials for shady areas. Of the several species native to North America, most are selections of *H. sanguinea* or hybrids thereof. Heucheras are easy to grow. They have small flowers in upright panicles but are more commonly grown for their dizzying array of foliage patterns. Some of the more popular selections are 'Amber Waves', 'Chocolate Veil', 'Mint Frost', 'Persian Carpet', 'Silver Scroll', and 'Velvet Knight'. Heucheras are also hybridized with foamflowers, *Tiarella cordifolia*, giving rise to intermediate plants called heucherellas. These low-growing plants with maplelike leaves are represented by cultivars such as 'Burnished Bronze', 'Kimono', 'Rosalie', and 'Viking Ship'. Zones 4–9.

Cranberry, *Vaccinium macrocarpon.*—The cranberry of commercial trade is a low-growing shrub that spreads by stolons. It has small, glossy leaves and astringent red berries. Several cultivars have been selected, and all have gardening potential. Zones 3–6.

Crested iris, *Iris cristata.*—This first-class small iris has white, light blue, or dark blue flowers with yellow falls. It spreads slowly across open areas and is easy to grow. Flowers are usually 5 inches tall, and foliage seldom exceeds 10 inches. Zones 4–8.

Foamflower, *Tiarella cordifolia.*—Similar to heucheras and heucherellas, foamflowers are smaller in size and make low, dense mats with sharply lobed maplelike leaves. 'Iron Butterfly', 'Jeepers Creepers', 'Spring Symphony', and 'Tigerstripe' have more colorful leaf patterns than the species. Zones 4–7.

Lingonberry, *Vaccinium vitis-idaea.*—Also known as mountain cranberry or cowberry, this is a choice groundcover of the blueberry family. The glossy leaves and pink to white flowers have typical urcelolate flowers. Improved cultivars are 'Red Pearl', 'Sanna', and 'Sussi'. Zones 4–5.

Mayflower, *Epigaea repens.*—Resembling a stoloniferous rhododendron, mayflower or trailing arbutus blooms in May and forms a low, flat mat in sterile, sandy areas. It is difficult to transplant from the wild and should be purchased in containers. Zones 5–8.

Oconee bells, *Shortia galacifolia.*—A plant whose native range is restricted to four counties in the Carolinas, Oconee bells has shiny, leathery, oval leaves and small white flowers in early spring. It is a classy plant for the cooler woodland garden. Zones 4–7.

Wakerobin, *Trillium erectum.*—Wakerobin is but one of a dozen or so trillium species that are adaptable to woodland gardens. The leaves, petals, and sepals are in threes. Flower colors range from white, yellow, pink, to shades of red. Zones 3–9.

Wandflower, *Galax urceolata.*—Also known as leatherleaf, this woody perennial has glossy, leathery leaves and tiny flowers on tall spikes. In sunny areas the winter foliage can be red or bronze. Zones 5–8.

Wild ginger, *Asarum shuttleworthii.*—An up-and-coming genus, wild gingers have thick, leathery leaves and fleshy flowers and roots that can be used to flavor stir-fry dishes. *Asarum nanaflora* 'Eco Décor', *A. shuttleworthii* 'Callaway' and 'Lazy K', *A. speciosum* 'Buxom Beauty' and 'Woodlanders Select' are among several cultivars that are now being cloned by micropropagation. Zones 4–9.

Wintergreen, *Gaultheria procumbens.*—Once used to produce oil of wintergreen, this diminutive evergreen mound has fragrant, lustrous foliage, pink to white flowers, and red berries. It does best in rich, damp soil and is a choice border plant. Zones 4–7.

SHRUBS

Arrowood, *Viburnum dentatum.*—As the name implies, the straight basal shoots of this 10-foot shrub were used as arrows by several indigenous American tribes. The plant is a strong grower and has flat-topped cymes composed of small white flowers followed by blue-black berries. The lustrous green leaves turn varying shades of yellow, orange, red, and purple in the fall. Cultivars include 'Autumn Jazz', half-size 'Blue Muffin', 'Chicago Lustre', red-leafed 'Red Feather', and 'Northern Burgundy'. American cranberrybush viburnum, *V. trilobum*, has maplelike leaves and is easy to grow. 'Alfredo' has superior red fall color, 'Redwing' has red-tinted new foliage, and 'Wentworth' has large red fruit. Zones 3–7.

Drooping leucothoe, *Leucothoë fontanesiana*.—Also known as fetterbush and very similar to coastal leucothoe, *L. axilaris*, this streamside shrub has arching limbs and lustrous leathery green leaves with serrate margins. Cultivars include 'Green Sprite, 'Mary Elizabeth', 'Scarletta', and variegated 'Rainbow' and 'Silver Run'. Zones 5–9.

Dusty zenobia, *Zenobia pulverulenta*.—Zenobia has arching branches, white urceolate flowers in May and June, and yellow to red fall foliage. 'Woodlanders Blue' is a choice selection with glaucous, blue-green foliage with rose and purple overtones. Zones 5–8.

Fringetree, *Chionanthus virginicus*.—Fringetree is a shrub to small tree with glossy dark green leaves. Fragrant white straplike flowers appear in droopy panicles in early May. It has good bark structure and in time will make a wide-spreading small tree. Zones 4–9.

Mountain laurel, *Kalmia latifolia*.—One of the best evergreen companion plants, mountain laurels have the same cultural requirements as azaleas. A wide range of new colors and growth habits has been developed in recent years. Selections are available with banded flowers, white flowers, red budded flowers, pink flowers, compact growth habits, and plants with narrow, willowlike leaves. Zones 4–9.

Mountain pieris, *Pieris floribunda*.—Pieris is a 4-foot dense evergreen shrub with short panicles of white flowers in April and May. The leaves are glossy, and the growth habit is stiff and formal. Pieris needs good drainage to thrive. Zones 4–6.

Ninebark, *Physocarpus opulifolius*.—Some plants are not well-known in gardens, and ninebark ranks at the top of that list. Ninebark is a multiple-stemmed 6-foot deciduous shrub with three-lobed leaves and fragrant white flowers borne in flat cymes. 'Diablo' is a new selection with dark red leaves. If planted near lime-green 'Nugget', the effect is very striking. Zones 2–7.

Oakleaf hydrangea, *Hydrangea quercifolia*.—In its larger forms, oak-leaf hydrangea is too vigorous for the typical azalea garden. Smaller selections such as 'Pee Wee' and 'Sykes' Dwarf' grow to less than half size. Winter wood is thick with peeling bark and the coarse, oaklike leaves provide a nice contrast to the finer leaves of azaleas. Zones 5–8.

Rosebay rhododendron, *Rhododendron maximum.*—In spite of its name, rosebay rhododendron usually has light pink to white flowers. It is easy to grow and makes a good backdrop for smaller azaleas. Other native rhododendron species include pink *R. carolinianaum, R. chapmanii, R. macrophyllum,* and *R. minus* and purple *R. catawbiense.* Zones 3–9.

Sandmyrtle, *Leiophyllum buxifolium.*—Sandmyrtle is a variable evergreen shrub, growing from nearly prostrate to 3 feet tall. It has small evergreen leaves and equally small white flowers. Plant it in an open sunny area with poor soil. Zones 5–7.

Sheep laurel, *Kalmia angustifolia.*—A distinct and appealing member of the laurel family, sheep laurel has small, buttonlike pink flowers and slightly drooping evergreen leaves. Cultivars 'Forever Green' and 'Wintergreen' have dark blue-green foliage, and compact 'Royal Dwarf' and 'Hammonasset' have rose-pink flowers. 'Candida' is a superior white selection. Zones 3–7.

Smooth hydrangea, *Hydrangea arborescens.*—Smooth hydrangea is a common roadside plant in the eastern half of the United States. The name arises from the smooth, light brown bark on its arching stems. It is best cut back to ground level in the winter, as flowers appear in the spring on new shoots. 'Annabelle', 'Samantha', and 'White Dome' have sterile snowball flower heads. Zones 3–7.

Summersweet, *Clethra alnifolia.*—Summersweet is a suckering shrub found from Maine to Florida. The small, fragrant white flowers appear in late summer on racemes up to 8 inches long. It is easy to grow, and leaves typically have good yellow fall color. 'Ann Bidwell' has large, upright candelabra-like panicles and a restrained growth habit. 'Creel's Calico' needs shade for best foliage variegation. 'Hummingbird' is compact. 'Ruby Spice' is the first true pink clethra, and the pink flowers open from bright ruby red buds. 'Sixteen Candles' is an improved seedling of 'Hummingbird'. *Clethra tomentosa* is a related southern species with downy white hairs on leaves and new growth. It is represented by 'Cottondale', a new selection with 14-inch racemes. Zones 5–9.

Sweetbells, *Leucothoë racemosa*.—This deciduous member of the leucothoe family is seldom seen in gardens but is easy to grow and has many fine attributes. Fragrant white flowers appear on typical racemes in April and May, and the leathery foliage turns burgundy red in the fall. Red-twig leucothoe, *L. recurva*, is a similar upland deciduous species. Zones 5-9.

Sweetshrub, *Calycanthus floridus*.—Sweetshrub is found from Virginia south to Florida. It has 1.5-inch, brownish red flowers with variable fruity fragrances. It typically grows as a 5-foot stoloniferous shrub. Compact cultivars such as 'Athens' with greenish yellow flowers and 'Michael Lindsey', which has dense, glossy foliage and good fragrance, bring this species several rungs up the ladder of popularity. Both are becoming more available and are well worth seeking out. Zones 4-9.

Sweetspire, *Itea virginica*.—Sweetspire has fragrant white flowers in 6-inch racemes and reaches a height of 4 feet. Leathery 4-inch dark green leaves turn shades of yellow, orange, and red in the fall. Cultivars include burgundy-leafed 'Henry's Garnet', compact 'Little Henry', soft pink 'Sarah 'Eve', and 'Saturnalia', which has yellow to orange to red fall foliage. Zones 5-9.

Winterberry, *Ilex verticillata*.—Grown primarily for fall leaf color and red berries, this deciduous holly is a favorite in gardens. Female cultivars produce huge quantities of berries if male pollinators such as 'Jim Dandy', 'Raritan Chief', or 'Southern Gentleman' are planted nearby. Female cultivars include 'Berry Nice', 'Cacapin', 'Jolly Red', 'Kennebago', 'Red Sprite', 'Stoplight, 'Winter Red', the compact orange 'Afterglow', and yellow 'Chrysocarpa'. Zones 3-9.

Witch alder, *Fothergilla major*.—One of the premiere flowering shrubs, witch alder has short bottlebrush racemes of white flowers and good fall color. 'Mt. Airy' has consistently good fall color. *Fothergilla gardenii* is smaller in all its parts and is represented by several cultivars. Zones 4-8.

Yellowroot, *Xanthorhiza simplicissima*.—This stoloniferous shrub fills a niche between groundcovers and shrubs. When scratched away, bark on stems and roots reveals bright yellow cambium, hence the name. If sited in a damp corner, the clump will fill in areas with dense foliage. Flowers are not showy, but fall leaf color is invariably bright yellow. Zones 4-9.

SMALL SHADE TREES

Dogwood, *Cornus florida*.—One of the three most popular small trees found in North America, this is truly a tree for all seasons. Dogwoods have good flowers, good fall color, and coarsely textured bark. Some of the more popular cultivars include white 'Cherokee Princess' and 'Cloud Nine' and red 'Cherokee Chief' and 'Cherokee Brave'. 'Plena' has double white flowers, and 'Purple Glory' has purple leaves and dark red flowers. Zones 5–9.

Red buckeye, *Aesculus pavia*.—Red buckeye makes an ideal small tree for shady woodlots. The five- to seven-lobed leaflets are glossy with distinct veins, and the red flowers are held in upright racemes. Bottlebrush buckeye, *A. parviflora*, is more shrublike and will need early pruning to grow into a small tree. Zones 4–8.

Redbud, *Cercis canadensis*.—Another of North America's premier small trees, redbud has year-round appeal. The foliage is heart shaped and leathery, and the pealike flowers give way to seedpods resembling edible snow peas. Improved cultivars include 'Appalachian Red' and 'Tennessee Pink'. 'Forest Pansy' has purple spring foliage. 'Royal White' has large flowers and is very floriferous. Zones 4–9.

Serviceberry, *Amelanchier arborea*.—Serviceberry trees have small but numerous feathery white flowers followed by edible blue berries. Superior cultivars include 'Autumn Brilliance', 'Coles Select', 'Forest Prince', and 'Princess Diana'. Zones 4–9.

Silverbell, *Halesia tetraptera*.—All the silverbells with four-winged seeds have now been lumped under *H. tetraptera*. Silverbell is usually a small tree found in damp streamside areas, and the white bell-shaped flowers are produced in abundance. 'Arnold Pink' has pale pink flowers and 'Wedding Bells' has numerous white flowers. 'Vestita' has a single trunk and velvety leaves. Similar *H. diptera* has two-winged seeds. Zones 5–9.

Sourwood, *Oxydendrum arboreum*.—Sourwood is the third member of our trio of superior small trees, the others being dogwood (*Cornus florida*) and redbud (*Cercis canadensis*). As common as weeds along roadsides in the Southeast, sourwood is seldom seen in gardens. It has an asymmetrical growth habit, graceful fingerlike racemes of small white flowers, and coarsely ridged bark. Fall foliage is bright shades of yellow, orange, and red. Zones 5–9.

EVERGREEN SCREENING TREES

American arborvitae, *Thuja occidentalis.*—The smaller selections of American arborvitae are the best screening evergreens for the East Coast. This species tolerates a wide range of soils and can be sheared if necessary. Narrow cultivars include 'Emerald', 'Hetz Wintergreen', 'Nigra', and 'Spiralis', whereas 'Techny' has a broader pyramidal shape. Zones 3–7.

Carolina cherrylaurel, *Prunus caroliniana.*—Cherrylaurel is a fast-growing member of the cherry family that tolerates sandy soil and is heat resistant. Seedlings can be sheared into a durable screen. 'Bright 'N Tight' is a compact, upright cultivar that needs little pruning and makes one of the better screens for the Deep South. Zones 7–9.

Florida leucothoe, *Agarista populifolia.*—This member of the leucothoe family recently had its name changed from *Leucothoë populifolia*. The tallest member of the family, Florida leucothoe is fast-growing, and a clump takes on bamboolike qualities as it ages. Height is to 15 feet, and the slowly stoloniferous habit will eventually make an impenetrable screen. Small urceolate flowers appear later than in the other species. Zones 6–9.

Inkberry, *Ilex glabra.*—Inkberry grows from Nova Scotia to Florida west to Mississippi. It has small shiny leaves and small black berries. Selections made for slower growth habit include 'Compacta', 'Nigra', 'Nova Scotia', 'Shamrock', and 'Viridis'. Zones 4–9.

Red cedar, *Juniperus virginiana.*—The old standby Christmas tree of years ago, red cedar is frequently seen along roadsides across the eastern states. 'Emerald Sentinel' and 'Burkii' are two choice upright selections. *Juniperus salicicola*, a southern extension of the above, is represented by 'Brodie', a selection with dense, emerald green foliage. Zones 3–9.

Smooth cypress, *Cupressus glabra.*—Smooth cypress is a tall conifer with scaly, bright blue-green foliage and smooth red-brown bark. The color of the needles makes an interesting contrast with the darker greens of other conifers and shrubs. 'Blue Ice' and 'Blue Pyramid' are compact selections with narrow growth habits. Zones 7–9.

Southern magnolia, *Magnolia grandiflora.*—Usually a tall, wide tree, smaller selections of southern magnolia can be used as screens. This classy tree has glossy leaves and large creamy white flowers. 'Little Gem' is the smallest selection and flowers sporadically throughout the summer and fall. 'Alta', 'Hasse', and 'Teddy Bear' are narrow cultivars with larger leaves. Zones 6–9.

White cedar, *Chamaecyparis thyoides.*—Found naturally in damp coastal areas, smaller selections of white cedar make interesting hedges with feathery fernlike foliage. Consider 'Fanfare' ('Shiva'), 'Red Star', and 'Yankee Blue'. Zones 4–7.

SCREENING VINES

As attractive as vines are, their spreading habit almost always leads to trouble if not sited properly. Fences in suburban yards, whether they are made of chain-link, split rail, or high-dollar stone or bricks, can be enhanced and softened with the addition of vines. They use a number of specialized holding mechanisms, but most can be grown directly on or tied to fences of many types. Vines are one of the few plants whose appearance can be enhanced by the use of hedge trimmers.

American wisteria, *Wisteria frutescens.*—Less invasive than its Asian counterparts, American wisteria also has smaller flower and a slower growth habit. 'Amethyst Falls' is bright purplish blue, and 'Nivea' has white flowers. 'Clara Mack', a cultivar of the similar Kentucky wisteria, *W. macrostachys*, has white flowers. Zones 5–9.

Carolina jasmine, *Gelsemium sempervirens.*—Carolina jasmine is one of our showiest vines. It has glossy evergreen leaves and canary yellow funnel-shaped flowers. Cultivars include double 'Pride of Augusta' and pale yellow 'Margarita'. Similar swamp jasmine, *G. rankinii*, is nonfragrant but produces flowers from spring to fall. Zones 6–9.

Crossvine, *Bignonia capreolata.*—Crossvine is a vigorous evergreen climber with trumpet-shaped flowers ranging from purple to red to orange. The name originates from the square cross-section of vine and the four leaflets that appear at each node. Cultivars include red 'Atrosanguinea' and orange 'Tangerine Beauty'. Zones 5–9.

Trumpet creeper, *Campsis radicans*.—Trumpet creeper is a vigorous, coarse, woody vine with large orange to red trumpet-shaped flowers. Because it is invasive, it is best planted on a post or low fence where it can be kept in bounds. Cultivars include 'Flava', 'Judy', and 'Variegata'. Zones 4–9.

Trumpet honeysuckle, *Lonicera sempervirens*.—A superior native vine, trumpet honeysuckle or coral honeysuckle has both entire and perfoliate leaves. It has narrow, trumpet-shaped flowers and climbs by twining its way up fenceposts. Cultivars selected for superior flower production include 'Alabama Crimson', 'Blanche Sandman', 'John Clayton', and yellow 'Sulphurea'. Zones 5–8.

Virginia creeper, *Parthenocissus quinquefolia*.—Virginia creeper, commonly called woodbine or woodvine, is a member of the grape family that is often confused with poison ivy. It climbs by tendrils tipped with sticky discs and has five leaflets per petiole. The flowers are fairly inconspicuous. 'Variegata' is one of the few cultivars available. Zones 4–9.

Virgin's bower, *Clematis virginiana*.—Virgin's bower, also known as woodvine, is a neglected but showy clematis that is occasionally seen in gardens. It has three to five leaflets and numerous fragrant 1-inch white flowers. With a little help on the way up, it will scramble across fences and nearby shrubs. Zones 4–8.

Wood vamp, *Decumaria barbara*.—Wood vamp is common but often goes unnoticed in the shady areas where it thrives. It has glossy leaves and small white flowers in cymes to 4 inches wide. It climbs by aerial rootlets and can scale rock walls and trees to 30 feet. Zones 5–7.

Chapter 6

Propagating Azaleas

Almost everyone who grows azaleas for any length of time will eventually develop an interest in propagating them. It has been said that when this urge appears, the hobby has turned to an obsession. Whether one's interest is to root a few cuttings or grow a batch of seedlings, the average gardener can do so with a little patience and imagination. In most instances propagating azaleas is a series of short steps with lots of downtime in between. By using the simple and somewhat passive methods presented here, azaleas can be propagated without imposing excessive time demands on the gardener.

Asexual Propagation

Also known as vegetative propagation, asexual propagation is a useful way to increase the number of plants of a favorite azalea or to propagate a plant found in the wild that has garden value or breeding potential. Asexual methods can vary from simple to complicated. As an example, the late August Kehr occasionally used a unique method to root evergreen azaleas. He placed a small amount of damp peat in a zip-top plastic bag and squeezed the peat into a lump in the bottom of the bag. He then stuck short azalea cuttings into the peat, blew into the bag to inflate it, and closed the bag. He attached the bag with a pin to the back of the curtains in his living room, which had a northern exposure. In a few weeks, white roots could be seen inside the bag. This method worked because it contained the key elements necessary to root cuttings: a moist rooting medium, high humidity, adequate light, and an even and moderate temperature inside the bag.

ROOTING CUTTINGS

Rooting softwood azalea cuttings is one of the most popular methods of propagation and one of the most frustrating. Some azaleas are not very difficult to root but getting the rooted cuttings to break dormancy in the spring can be problematic. The traditional method involves the use of a mist system with automatic controls and a greenhouse or other structure that needs to be monitored closely. There are simple, low-volume methods of rooting softwood cuttings that can be very effective, although they are somewhat slower.

One of the best methods is to use transparent plastic boxes with close-fitting lids (see Figure 11D). An ideal box would measure about 16 inches long × 9 inches wide × 6 inches deep. Fill the box half full of damp, unmilled sphagnum moss (not peat moss), available in compressed cubic-foot bags at most garden centers. Dry sphagnum absorbs cold water very slowly but warm water almost immediately. The sphagnum should be squeezed of excess water and spread evenly in the box to a depth of 3 inches. Although sphagnum has natural fungicidal qualities, to prevent mold all extraneous dry grass stems and blades should be clipped from the top layer prior to applying the seeds. An alternative medium is equal parts of finely ground pine bark, peat, and perlite.

Softwood cuttings, approximately 4 inches in length, should be taken in the spring. As soon as the new shoots harden, usually by late May, cut the ends at an angle and dip in a rooting powder such as Hormodin #3. Stick them in the rooting medium on 1-inch centers and cover the box with a white plastic trash bag. Place the bagged box on a table or other protected outdoor site in an area with high shade. If the light level is too high, the box may need to be covered with shade cloth. At no time should the box be exposed to direct sunlight. By late fall the cuttings should be rooted. This can be checked by pulling gently on a few cuttings to feel for resistance created by the formation of roots. Rooted cuttings are very prone to bark split during extremely low winter temperatures. To prevent damage, the bagged box of rooted cuttings should be moved into a cool, dimly lit inside area during the colder months or placed in a heated or unheated greenhouse or a cool basement. In early May of the following year, the rooted cuttings should be placed in a raised bed or in small pots for at least one growing season prior to moving to permanent sites.

DIVISION

Division is a method that has long been used to propagate azaleas. If the area around a large azalea is examined closely, there will usually be one or more shoots with small roots attached that can be cut from the root-ball. Provided the division taken is small, this process does not damage the parent pant. If the division has an adequate number of roots, it can be planted in a permanent location or can be placed in a holding bed or container for one growing season until more roots develop.

LAYERING

Layering is a slow but sure method of propagating a favorite plant. Excavate a small hole near the base of the azalea and bend a small, flexible limb into it. Cover the limb with a layer of soil and leaf mold and place a large rock over the limb to hold it in place (Figure 8A). Scatter ½ cup of granular fertilizer over and around the layer to speed up the rooting process. Depending on the species and other factors, the limb should root well enough to be removed from the plant in one to two years. After removal it can either be planted in a permanent site or grown for a year in a temporary bed or container.

POT LAYERING

Pot layering is a modification of layering that provides for quicker rooting (Figure 8B). Split a sturdy container down one side and across the bottom to the drain hole. Pull a limb into and out of the pot via the drain hole, overlap the cut sides of the pot at the top, and secure to a stake with two wood screws. The pot should then be filled with a moisture-retaining mix, such as moss from nearby logs, damp sphagnum, or finely ground pine bark. Sprinkle 1 teaspoon of slow-release granular fertilizer on top of the medium and water frequently with dilute liquid fertilizer.

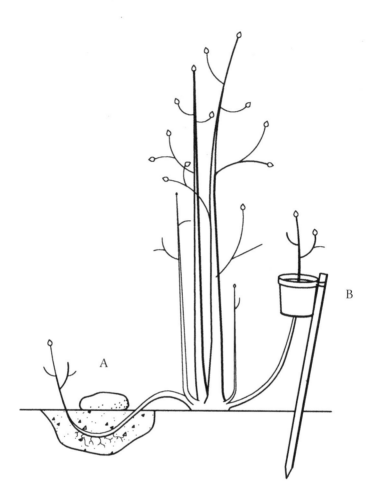

Figure 8. (A) A ground layer and (B) a high-rise pot layer are two easy ways to propagate small quantities of azaleas and other shrubs. Drawing by Allen Cantrell

Limbs up to ¼ inch in diameter will root in a few months using this method. The same method will work with the pot on the ground, provided it is attached to a stake to prevent critters from turning it over.

AN ALTERNATIVE METHOD

Allen Cantrell, a patent draftsman who did the drawings in this book, is an azalea collector from Chesnee, South Carolina. Allen has developed an alternative method of vegetative propagation that is very effective (Figure 9). He has collected azaleas from both coasts and has tried the method on all azalea species. Due to his frequent long trips, Allen needed a method that would allow him to propagate azaleas with unusual flowers, his specialty, without having to revisit the plant a second time. Root cuttings, rooted layers, and rooted or unrooted heel cuttings will all work with this method. The best time to take root cuttings is late winter through May. No hormones are used. The following is a summary of his methods:

Dig around the base of a plant to find a suitable size root from ¾ inch down to the size of a pencil. If the root is large, follow it out to smaller side roots. Cut the root 6 inches or longer, and keep small feeder roots attached. For proper orientation when potting, make a straight cut on the large end of the root and an angle cut on the small end of the root.

Until potted, place root cuttings in a plastic bag with wet pine bark to prevent dehydration. Pot the cuttings in a #3 plastic container filled with equal parts of ground pine bark, peat, and perlite. Leave ½ to ¾ inch of each cutting above the soil line.

Water the potted cuttings thoroughly. Place a stake in the container and enclose all in a white trash bag. Some excess water needs to be left in the bag, which will wick upward through the peat to keep it uniformly moist. Close the bag with a twist-tie.

Place the bagged cuttings in a bright shaded area away from direct sunlight.

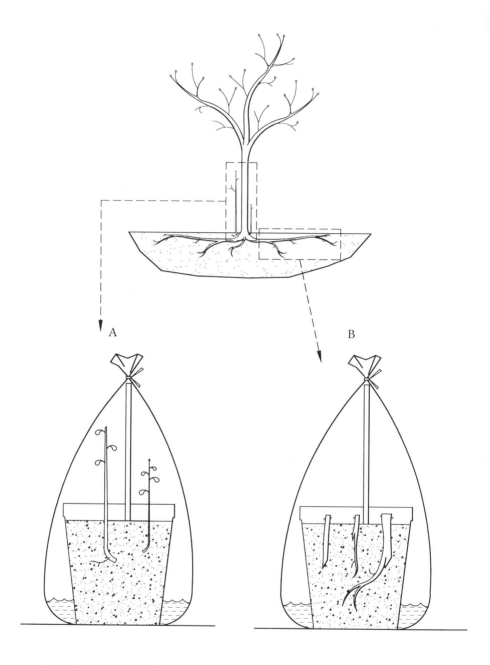

Figure 9. Allen Cantrell's alternative propagation method works well on (A) heel cuttings as well as (B) root cuttings. Never expose the bagged pots to direct sunlight. Drawing by Allen Cantrell

The exposed ends of the roots should start forming small red
bumps in about 6 weeks. These will grow into new shoots
up to 3 inches long the first summer.

As the shoots begin to elongate, tear small holes in the bag to
gradually lower the humidity. After the shoots have
elongated fully, remove the bag from the container to
lower the temperature to prevent mold diseases.

The containers can be left out the first winter or placed in a
cold frame or shade house. No fertilizer is used the first
summer.

MICROPROPAGATION

Micropropagation is a method primarily used in large laboratories. As
the technology improves, however, its use may become commonplace to
the hobbyist. In simple terms, a dormant vegetative or flower bud or a
small piece of an actively growing vegetative shoot is removed from the
plant to be cloned. If a dormant bud is used, the scales are removed and
the embryonic bud is excised, sterilized, and placed in a test tube filled
with agar, growth hormones, and carbohydrates. In a few weeks the bud
(or piece of shoot) will begin to send up several tiny shoots complete with
leaves, and the inside of the test tube will begin to resemble a miniature
chia pet. These shoots are exact duplicates of the parent plant in all
respect except they lack roots. As soon as the shoots have elongated to 1
inch or so, they are clipped from the parent tissue and stuck in a moist
medium where, due to seedling-like juvenility, they will produce roots in
a matter of days. Now equipped with roots, the new plants will respond
quickly to fertilizer. As they grow, the tops can be clipped again and these
shoots will also form roots. Within months thousands of clones of a selection can be grown and handled as easily as seedlings.

Sexual Propagation

Unlike vegetative propagation, which simply involves cloning one plant
into several identical plants, sexual propagation is a way for the gardener
to obtain seedlings that will show considerable variation. To most hobby-

ists, it is the variation found in seedlings that makes plant breeding interesting and worthwhile.

BASIC GENETICS

Although a thorough understanding of genetics is not essential to breeding azaleas, some basic knowledge is useful. In most species of azaleas, an ovule (unfertilized seed) contains 13 chromosomes and a grain of pollen contains 13 chromosomes. At the time of fertilization, pollen enters the pistil via the stigma, grows down the style, enters the ovulary (immature seedpod), and fertilizes the ovules, a process that takes less than two hours. The resulting seeds and seedlings thus contain 26 chromosomes per plant cell. Azaleas species that have 26 chromosomes in two matched sets of 13 (AA) are referred to as diploids ($2n = 26$). *Rhododendron calendulaceum* and *R. canadense* have twice the usual number of chromosomes and are referred to as tetraploids ($2n = 52$). *Rhododendron canadense* is an autotetraploid with 52 chromosomes in two matched sets of 26 (AA/AA), whereas *R. calendulaceum* is an allotetraploid with 52 chromosomes in two unmatched sets of 26 (AA/BB). This derived species is unusual in that it carries two complete genomes, one most likely from *R. cumberlandense* (AA) and one probably from *R. prinophyllum* (BB). When *R. calendulaceum* is crossed with a diploid such as *R. periclymenoides*, some of the resulting seedlings will be fertile and some will be sterile triploids ($2n = 39$).

Rhododendron occidentale is typically a diploid, but the larger-flowered forms have 52 chromosomes and in some instances are hexaploids ($2n = 78$). Due to genetic incompatibilities beyond chromosome numbers, *R. canadense* and *R. vaseyi* have not yet produced viable seeds when crossed with each other or with any other American species. *Rhododendron calendulaceum* and *R. occidentale*, however, will cross with each other and with all other American species with five anthers. Additionally, all diploid species with five anthers will cross with each other in all pairwise combinations, which gives ample hybridizing opportunities.

SETTING GOALS

There may be valid reasons for germinating seeds of unknown parentage, but the time will be better spent growing seedlings from a cross that has been made with some plan in mind. If the breeder is interested in growing seedlings that will bloom in a wide range of colors, a good first-step is to cross one of the orange or red species with a fragrant white or pink species. The late Joe Gable observed many years ago that the seedlings of a cross between *Rhododendron calendulaceum* and *R. periclymenoides* looked as if a group of monkeys had painted the flowers. If the breeder is interested in yellow flowers only, there may be some benefit to be gained in vigor by crossing two yellow azaleas of different species, such as *R. calendulaceum* with *R. austrinum*. If the breeder is more ambitious, there are azaleas available in the trade that can provide more interesting results in the same length of time, and a review of the cultivar list in chapters 7 and 8 is recommended.

COLLECTING AND STORING POLLEN

Many successful crosses have been made between two plants that bloom at the same time or a few days apart. This practice, however, places severe limits on the breeder with regard to potential outcomes. Pollen will remain viable at room temperature for only a few days, so knowing how to collect, desiccate, and freeze it for later use is recommended.

Pollen is best collected and stored in #2 gelatin capsules, which can be purchased at pharmacies or health food stores. Because they are sensitive to moisture, both from humidity and perspiration, capsules should always be kept dry. When ready to collect pollen, remove the capsule top and set it aside. Hold the long bottom half upright between thumb and middle finger and use the index finger to cut the anthers from the filaments that have been moved into place with the other hand. Collect anthers with visible pollen, if possible. When an adequate number of anthers have been collected, preferably several dozen, replace the top and close the capsule with a thin strip of masking tape. Fold the end of the strip of tape on itself to form a label. Label the tag end with date and type of pollen.

At this point the pollen is ready to desiccate. Place a ½ inch of desiccating crystals or powdered coffee creamer in a small container such as a 35-mm film canister. Cover the desiccant with cotton and place the capsule on top of the cotton. Close the container and store at room temperature for twenty-four hours to allow the crystals to pull the water from the pollen through the capsule wall, then place the container in a freezer until needed. The pollen will thaw as soon as taken out to make a cross and can be refrozen after use. Pollen desiccated and stored correctly will last for several years, but it is better to replace it every two or three years.

HAND POLLINATION

Hand pollination, also referred to as cross-pollination or simply making a cross, is another easy process. Before making a cross, it might be helpful to watch a bumblebee, one of the primary pollinators of azaleas. The bumblebee, true to its name, will crash unceremoniously into a truss of flowers to collect nectar. The bee's hairy legs will be loaded with pollen from previous landings. As it clambers across the flowers (Figure 10), some of the pollen will find its way onto the stigmas, resulting in fertilization. By duplicating the action of the bee, a cross can be made in which the breeder, unlike the bee, knows the source of the pollen and is one essential key to successful plant breeding.

To make a cross select a truss with several fully open flowers on the plant to be used as the pod parent. (Some breeders prefer to expose stigmas of unopened flowers to insure that they are free of pollen. This is a good method, but in many instances the stigmas may not yet be sticky and thus not receptive to pollen.) Remove any unopened flowers on the truss with small scissors to prevent later formation of seedpods from an unknown pollen source. Reverse the process of collecting pollen by tipping the pistil of a flower with one hand into the opened capsule containing the pollen. Move the stigma around inside the capsule to make contact with the pollen. If the pollen in not visible, hold the capsule by its tape tag and thump sharply to dislodge pollen that may be hidden inside the anthers. Another method is to dab a small artist's brush into the capsule and then brush it across the stigmas. After making a cross, the brush should be cleaned first with alcohol then with water and dried before being used again.

After a cross is made on all opened flowers of a truss, label and tie a small tag on the stem just below the pollinated flowers to indicate the source of pollen. In two or three days the pollinated flowers will begin to slide from the ovularies, which will begin to swell into seedpods in a few weeks if the cross was successful. The pods will continue to swell to maximum size over the next few months. On some species the green pods will

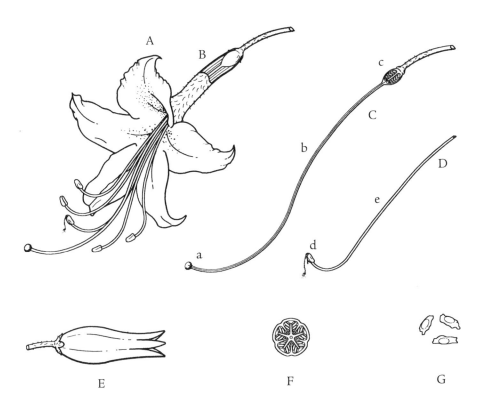

Figure 10. A typical azalea flower includes (A) the corolla; (B) the tube;
(C) the pistil, including (a) stigma, (b) style, and (c) ovulary; and
(D) the stamen, including (d) pollen-containing anther and (e) filament.
A seedpod with calyx and pedicel attached is shown (E) enlarged and
(F) in cross-section, and (G) seeds are shown further enlarged. Drawing
by Allen Cantrell

look like miniature bananas (*R. periclymenoides*) and on others like miniature footballs (*R. arborescens*).

CLEANING SEEDS

A seedpod contains five chambers, each potentially filled with viable seeds. As soon as the tagged pods begin to change color from green to bronze, usually by early October, they should be collected before the pods split and the seeds begin to drop naturally. After the pods are removed, place them in a bowl and dry for a few days at room temperature. The pods are now ready for seed removal.

To remove the seeds, break a pod in half, hold it over a sheet of white paper, and twist the pod half between thumb and forefinger. Hopefully the pod will crush and the seeds drop out. If not, gently crack the pod half with a small pair of pliers and try again. In some cases the pod may have to be torn apart and the seeds teased from the chambers with a toothpick. With the exception of *R. arborescens*, which has wingless, granular seeds, azalea seeds are easy to overlook as they are imbedded in tiny, irregular brown wings that look like miniature cornflakes. Separate the seeds from the pod debris and store in a small envelope until needed. Seeds will stay viable for many years.

GROWING SEEDLINGS

A 48-inch two-bulb fluorescent light suspended above a shelf in a heated basement or pantry makes a small but very efficient germination area (Figure 11). Room temperature should be from 65 to 75°F. Clear or semitransparent plastic utility boxes make perfect, low-maintenance growing chambers for the seedlings. The boxes can be of various sizes and shapes, but should have lids that fit fairly tightly. A good size is 16 inches long × 9 inches wide × 6 inches deep. The light should be suspended from 6 to 8 inches above the box tops to allow room for the lids to be removed to add fertilizer, and the fixture should be plugged into a timer and set to eight hours per day.

One of the best germinating mediums for seeds is sphagnum moss, which can be purchased in cubic-foot bales. Another popular medium is equal parts of finely ground pine bark, sand, and perlite. The medium should be damp but not excessively wet. If water collects in the bottom

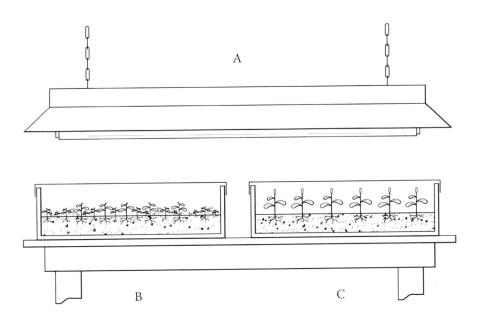

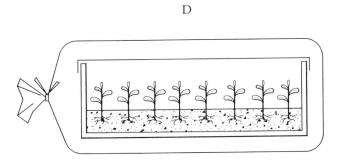

Figure 11. A typical seedling germination area consists of (A) a light source, (B) a germinating box, and (C) a transplant box. (D) Softwood cuttings can be rooted in the same type of box outside without lights. Drawing by Allen Cantrell

of the box, bore a hole at one corner to allow it to drain off onto paper towels placed under the box.

For maximum growth, seeds should be planted in October or November. Sprinkle the seeds from one cross in a row on top of the medium (do not cover the seeds) and label the row on a strip of plastic, which should be stuck between the medium and the container at the back of the row. Fertilizing is best done with a new or discarded spray bottle, making sure any previous contents have been removed. A very small amount of powdered azalea fertilizer (⅛ teaspoon per 32 ounces of water) should be added to the bottle. If mold appears later, add a pinch of fungicidal powder to the fertilizer. As soon as the seeds are sown, thoroughly mist the top of the medium with the fertilizer mix and replace the top. With a little luck the only time the top of the box will have to be removed is to fertilize lightly every week or so. Moisture will soon collect on the underside of the top, but it will drain back down the side, creating the high humidity needed for seed germination.

In a few days the seedlings will begin to germinate, first showing cotyledon then true leaves. When the seedlings have two or three sets of leaves they are ready to be picked off and placed into a second box. Even though they are tender, simply pull a seedling up slowly and its roots will slide from the moss. Use a toothpick to make holes 1 inch on center in the medium of the second box, and push the bare roots of the seedlings into the holes. Small balls of moss make handy plugs to push in the holes to anchor the seedlings. Some minor root damage may occur, but the seedlings will recover. If using plug trays or peat cups, consider placing three or four seedlings in each cell. The seedlings can be broken apart later when they are ready to be transplanted to an outside bed.

After some of the seedlings have been transplanted into the second box, the germinating box can be emptied and recycled as a transplant box to hold the remaining seedlings. Depending on spacing, a transplant box can hold up to 200 seedlings. After the seedlings get over the shock of being transplanted, the tops of the transplant boxes should be raised and eventually removed to allow the seedlings to become acclimated to a less humid environment. As the seedlings pick up speed, they can be pruned with small scissors to force lateral branching. If a seedling looks particularly interesting, cut the top out and use a toothpick to stick it between the medium at the front of the box so the cut end is visible through the plastic. Due to the juvenility of seedlings, roots will appear like magic in a few days. During the next few months, the seedlings should be watered every few days with the water-fertilizer mix. If they have to be neglected, the lids can be put back in place for several weeks without damage. The only attention needed until spring is to insure that the medium does not become dry and that the temperature stays within the comfort range.

Another method for growing seedlings is to transplant them into a commercial domed Styrofoam or plastic unit that comes equipped with compressed peat plugs. These are available at garden centers and through mail-order sources and are very easy to use.

TRANSPLANTING SEEDLINGS

By early May the transplant boxes should be filled to the tops with healthy seedlings ready to move outdoors. They should be potted up individually into 3-inch square pots filled with the peat, sand, and perlite mix and placed in a protected area such as a shade house.

One problem with growing seedlings outside in pots is that the medium tends to dry out quickly. An alternate method is to build a raised bed made of dry-stacked 6- or 8-inch concrete blocks 4 feet wide × 8 feet long × 24 inches high. Begin by clearing a flat area under high shade and covering with one or more layers of plastic sheeting to prevent tree roots from invading the bed. Stack three courses of blocks on the plastic. No mortar is needed if the blocks are overlapped every 8 inches, although tubes of concrete glue can easily be applied between the blocks for added security. Fill the bottom two-thirds of the bed with coarse pine bark and top with 4 to 6 inches of finely ground pine bark. Seedlings should be kept there for at least one growing season before being planted into permanent locations.

FERTILIZING SEEDLINGS

Small transplanted azaleas will benefit from frequent watering with dilute liquid or powdered fertilizer. This should be done with a metered siphon sprayer attached to a garden hose. Avoid using nonsiphon sprayers because they apply fertilizer at uneven rates. Another method is to use a 2-gallon pail of water to which a heaping teaspoon of quick-dissolving azalea fertilizer has been added. Err on the side of caution because azalea seedlings are sensitive to fertilizer. As fall approaches, hold off on water and fertilizer to allow the seedlings to harden off before the colder winter months.

OVERWINTERING SEEDLINGS

Unlike rooted cuttings, small seedlings can overwinter with less chance of being damaged by freezing weather. A simple method is to cover the seedlings in the raised bed with a thick layer of pine limbs in late fall. Another method is to insert flexible black plastic water pipes into the holes in the blocks to form bows like a covered wagon. Cover the bows with translucent plastic to form a small greenhouse. During periods of warm weather in winter or spring, the plastic can be pulled back on warm days to prevent the seedlings from breaking dormancy too early. The plastic cover should be completely removed in the spring when the danger of hard freezes has passed.

AZALEA GENERATIONS

In November 2001 Nick Anastos germinated a flat of *Rhododendron austrinum* seeds inside his house in a plastic box under lights. In May 2002 the seedlings were taken outside, separated, and planted in 4-inch square rose pots. The pots were top-dressed with ½ teaspoon of granular slow-release fertilizer and the azaleas received an application of dilute liquid fertilizer every day or so from a metered sprayer attached to garden hose. By late fall about half of the fifty seedlings, not yet a year old, had set some flower buds for the following year. In April 2003, seventeen months after germination, they bloomed. This was possible due to two factors: this species is vigorous and usually sets buds earlier than most and they were given close attention and constant fertilizer. The remainder of the seedlot will bloom in the spring of 2004 at the age of two and a half years. Given the same care, most species can be enticed to bloom in three and a half years from seeds. Nonfragrant red and orange species usually take a year longer to bloom than fragrant white, pink, and yellow species.

Chapter 7

Improving Azaleas: Past to Present

In 1680 John Bannister, an English missionary, sent seeds of *Rhododen-dron viscosum* to Bishop Henry Compton in England. Seeds of *R. pericly-menoides*, *R. canescens*, *R. canadense*, and *R. calendulaceum* found their way to England by the late 1700s. By the early 1800s these azaleas, as well as *R. luteum* from Europe, reached Ghent, Belgium, and the azalea-hybridiz-ing craze reached full tilt. The Ghent azaleas, as they came to be called, eventually incorporated other species into a group of upright, hardy aza-leas that came in a wide range of colors. Concurrent with the Ghent breed-ing program, other Belgian breeders focused on developing azaleas with larger flowers by crossing two Asian species, *R. molle* and *R. japonicum*, with *R. viscosum*. This group, which came to be known as Mollis Hybrids, had larger flowers than the Ghents, but they were less hardy.

In 1870 Anthony Waterer at Knap Hill Nursery in England, crossed the Ghent azaleas with *R. molle* and began the Knap Hill azaleas. From there plants were sent to Lionel de Rothchild in Exbury, England, where he began the Exbury azalea program. Material from the Knap Hill Nurs-ery also found its way to Christchruch, New Zealand, where selections were crossed with *R. calendulaceum*, *R. viscosum*, *R. molle*, and *R. occidentale* from the West Coast of the United States. All of the various New Zealand breeding programs were eventually consolidated into Ilam azaleas, a ven-ture that is still underway today.

As these improved hybrid azaleas spread, some were sent to the United States. Breeding programs began here and continued to focus on

91

large flowers with heavy substance, bright colors, fragrance, and adaptability to specific growing conditions. In the mid-1900s azalea fanciers on the East Coast began to realize that the advances made in the hybridizing programs in Belgium, England, and New Zealand had produced many plants that were not hardy in the cold Northeast or that languished in the heat of the South. To correct these problems they began various breeding programs that incorporated some of the hybrids developed overseas or in some cases used only local species. A look at a few of the breeders gives an idea of the various approaches that were taken.

Frank Abbott, a Vermont heating contractor and woodcarver, developed an interest in azaleas in the 1920s. He began by crossing pink *Rhododendron prinophyllum*, a very hardy local species, with one of the hardier red Mollis azaleas and developed several fragrant, bright pink selections. He also crossed *R. calendulaceum* with *R. prinophyllum* and selected and named several seedlings from this cross. Many of his azaleas can be found growing in his hometown of Saxtons Mill.

George Beasley, a farmer by trade, liked to spend his leisure time trout fishing in the mountains of northern Georgia. There he developed an appreciation for azaleas that eventually led to the founding of Transplant Nursery, which is still in operation today. His focus was on propagating superior wild species and hybrids, though he later began a breeding program involving *Rhododendron austrinum* and a Choptank azalea similar to 'Marydel'. From this cross he named several cultivars that are still in production.

S. D. Coleman, a Georgia pharmacist, sold his drugstore and went into the nursery business, first growing camellias and evergreen azaleas. Later his interest changed to deciduous azaleas, and he created a 50-acre naturalistic garden called Coleman's Native Azalea Trail, which was far ahead of its time in scope. He became friends with Cason and Virginia Callaway, and his azalea trail had an impact on the development of Callaway Gardens. He grew azalea seedlings by the truckload, which were shipped to various places, and he named several that can be found in private collections today.

Leonard Frisbie of Oregon was perhaps the most persistent collector of azaleas. Leonard became enamored with *Rhododendron occidentale* and spent the better part of a decade collecting unusual specimens of this colorful species. In the spring and summer he took bus trips into California and hiked from town to town, visiting farms and getting permission to tag and catalog unusual plants. In the winter he returned in his Jeep, towing a trailer, and dug the plants. His work was the first systematic study of this species.

Fred Galle of Georgia did some azalea breeding. He is best known, however, for the three books he wrote on azaleas and hollies and the role he played in the development of Callaway Gardens. While serving as their horticultural director, he bought azaleas by the thousand from nearby nurseries and planted them along the four-mile loop drive. As a result of his efforts the gardens are credited with having one of the world's largest deciduous azalea collections.

David Leach of Pennsylvania and later Ohio was best known for his writing on and work with rhododendrons, but he developed two groups of hardy azaleas. He, like other before and after, was impressed with the vivid colors of the hybrid swarms of *Rhododendron arborescens* × *R. cumberlandense* of the southern Appalachians. The Madison Group consisted of cutting-grown and seedling selections from Gregory Bald in Tennessee and Copper Bald in North Carolina. A few selections from this group were later crossed with *R. prunifolium* to create the July Group. They combined the hardiness of the Madison Group with the late flowers of the plumleaf azalea.

Edmund Mezitt, a friend of Frank Abbott and owner of Weston Nurseries in Massachusetts, began crossing *Rhododendron prinophyllum* with some of the Abbott Hybrids in the 1950s, but his focus soon changed to summer-blooming azaleas. He crossed seedlings of *R. prunifolium* that were sent to him by Fred Galle at Callaway Gardens with *R. arborescens*, *R. cumberlandense*, *R. viscosum*, and a few of the smaller-flowered Ghent azaleas. The plants bloomed from early June into September and most were fragrant. This line of work is still continuing at the nursery today.

Britt Smith and Frank Mossman of Oregon took a very detailed and systematic approach to examining the intricacies of the many variations in *Rhododendron occidentale*. During the better part of sixteen years they scoured the range of the western azalea and collected cuttings and pollen from the many unusual plants they found. They also made many controlled crosses, adding even more variation to the species.

In 1996 the South King County Arboretum was founded, with its mission being the relocation of the large Smith-Mossman collection to a central location. In 2000 the project was completed with the dedication and opening of the Smith-Mossman Western Azalea Display Garden in King County, Washington.

Aaron Varnadoe, a southern Georgia farmer, started a breeding program that focused on the rootability of *Rhododendron austrinum*. He crossed that species with *R. canescens* and later with *R. flammeum* and developed numerous heat-tolerant cultivars that were easy to root. Many of his selections have flowers that resemble *R. austrinum* but that come in a wide range of colors. He sold plants to the public, and many of his seedlings and selections found their way to Callaway Gardens, where they can still be seen today.

Ongoing Improvement Efforts

Today a few nurseries are continuing to improve azaleas that are adapted to regional growing conditions. Some are using Exbury azaleas to produce large flowers, whereas others are concentrating only on local species and their hybrids.

Aromi Hybrids.—Eugene Aromi, a retired Alabama college professor, began a breeding program using a heat-tolerant Exbury azalea crossed with *Rhododendron austrinum*. His goal was to develop plants with large, fragrant flowers that could withstand the heat and humidity of the Gulf States of the South. His cultivars come in various shades of yellow, orange, and salmon, with some having bright yellow or orange blotches.

Confederate Series.—Tom Dodd III began a breeding program by sending pollen of *Rhododendron austrinum* to a friend, who crossed it with an Exbury azalea. His goal was to develop heat-tolerant plants with thick foliage and large, fragrant flowers in a wide range of colors. Of the dozen or so he has released to date, all are named after people associated with the Civil War, or in his terms, "the recent unpleasantness."

Lazy K azaleas.—Lazy K Nursery was established in 1958 by Ernest Koone Jr. as a continuation of a family farm in continuous operation since 1827. Early in its existence an emphasis was placed on native plants of the Southeast, with a particular interest in deciduous azaleas. The nursery established a relationship with Fred Galle and the founders of Callaway Gardens and provided many of the plants that can be seen there today. Ernest Koone III, the present owner, has made the nursery into one of the largest specializing in American azaleas. Due to the large quantity of seedlings he grows, in recent years he has begun selecting superior plants, both species and hybrids, and is producing an increasing number of them.

Maid in the Shade azaleas.—Continuing the breeding program developed by George Beasley, Jeff and Lisa Beasley, owners of Transplant Nursery, introduced the first line of azaleas using a trademarked label and logo. This colorful group of plants contains several species selections as well as hybrids. Their innovative marketing and distribution plan has moved azaleas several rungs up the ladder of popularity.

Northern Lights Series.—Harold Pellett, a professor at the University of Minnesota, continues to work on the Northern Lights Series, a very hardy group of azaleas that can withstand temperatures as low as −40°F. These azaleas were developed by crossing two Asiatic species, *R. molle* and *R. japonicum*, with *R. atlanticum* and *R. prinophyllum*. Colors range from white to yellow to shades of pink, salmon, and rose. The series also contains several sterile *R. canadense* × *R. japonicum* hybrids, a cross that is very difficult to make.

Pastel Series.—Robert McCartney, owner of renowned Woodlanders Nursery, has probably traveled more miles on foot looking for azaleas and other plants than any of his counterparts. Living in an area rich in wild azaleas, he has collected a large number of wild *R. alabamense* × *R. canescens* × *R. flammeum* hybrids and propagates them in a numbered Pastel Series. The plants are easy to grow and do well in the South, as well as into the mid-Atlantic States.

Summer Series.—Wayne Mezitt, co-owner of Weston Nurseries, continues to breed and introduce azaleas from the program started by his father. As a group, the plants bloom from June to September. Most are fragrant and they come in a wide range of colors, with some having attractive, blue-green foliage. Although some of the plants are of Ghent azalea lineage, their average flower size and typical growth habit allows them to meet the conditions for inclusion in the cultivar list of American azaleas.

Available Azalea Cultivars

The following list contains the majority of American azalea cultivars available at wholesale and retail nurseries and from mail-order sources. The names in parentheses are of the person(s) who named the plant, and if known, the name of the nursery that introduced the plant. Shrub height represents the expected growth rate of a two-gallon container plant after ten years in a typical garden situation. A selection grown from seeds is designated by "S" and if collected in the wild by "CW". Bloom time is indicated within the average month of bloom, which will be affected by altitude, latitude, and several other factors. Northern limits of hardiness are estimates based on species and hybrid parentage (see Appendix D for hardiness zone temperature ranges).

'Alba' (unknown), *R. canadense.*—White flowers instead of the usual lavender or purple, otherwise typical for the species, 4 feet, CW, May, zone 3.

'Anna's Smile' (Mezitt/Weston), *R. arborescens* ×.—Fragrant gold-blotched pink flowers age to peach pink, glossy rounded foliage, 5 feet, S, June, zone 5.

'Apricot Glow' (Mezitt/Weston), *R. arborescens* × *R. prunifolium.*—Fragrant apricot-pink, 5 feet, S, July, zone 5.

'BAN Select' (Jaynes/Broken Arrow), *R. atlanticum* × *R. calendulaceum.*—Pink and yellow ages to darker pink, dark glossy foliage, 5 feet, S, May, zone 5.

'Betty Cummins' (Lewis), *R. viscosum.*—Fragrant pink, reflexed petals, semiglossy foliage, upright growth habit, 5 feet, CW, May, zone 5.

'Biltmore' (Biltmore Estate), *R. atlanticum* × *R. canescens.*—Fragrant white, dark foliage, upright growth habit, 6 feet, CW, May, zone 5.

'Bonbon' (Mezitt/Weston), (*R. cumberlandense* × *R. viscosum*) × *R. arborescens.*—Fragrant pink, blue-green foliage, 5 feet, S, June, zone 5.

'Camilla's Blush' (Beasley/Transplant), *R. canescens.*—Fragrant soft pink, 6 feet, S, April, zone 6.

'Camp's Red' (Skinner), *R. cumberlandense.*—Red, upright habit to 6 feet, CW, June, zone 5.

'Chauncy Beadle' (Biltmore Estate), *R. cumberlandense* × *R. viscosum.*—Deep pink, yellow blotch, hairy stems, semidwarf to 4 feet, CW, June, zone 5.

'Chickasaw' (Towe-Anastos/Lazy K), *R. calendulaceum* × *R. periclymenoides.*—Light salmon ages to bright salmon rose, large flowers, ribbed foliage, 6 feet, CW, April–May, zone 5.

'Chocolate Drop' (Koone/Lazy K), *R. canescens.*—Fragrant white, leaves emerge chocolate red and later age to dark green, 6 feet, S, April, zone 6.

'Choice Cream' (Galle), *R. atlanticum* × *R. austrinum.*—Fragrant light yellow with gold blotch, pink tubes, small foliage, 5 feet, S, April–May, zone 5.

'Coleman's Sunshine' (Coleman), same as 'Rushin's Austrinum', *R. atlanticum* × *R. austrinum.*—Fragrant yellow with dark gold blotch carries as bright yellow, clumping growth habit, semiglossy convex foliage, 5 feet, S, April, zone 5.

'Clyo Red' (McCartney/Woodlanders), *R. canescens* × *R. flammeum.*—Dark cherry pink, 5 feet, CW, April, zone 6.

'Dawn at the River' (Beasley/Transplant), *R. calendulaceum.*—Opens yellow, ages to orange then red, all colors show together, 6 feet, CW, May, zone 5.

'Deep Rose' (Mezitt/Weston), *R. arborescens* ×.—Fragrant dark pink, dense growth habit, dark green foliage, 5 feet, S, June, zone 4.

'Delaware Blue' (Hill), *R. viscosum.*—Fragrant white, glaucous blue-green foliage, upright growth habit, 6 feet, CW, May, zone 5.

'Doctor Helen' (Sams/Lazy K), *R. calendulaceum* × *R. canescens.*—Opens white, ages to bright rose, vigorous, floriferous, 6 feet, CW, April, zone 5.

'Earl's Gold' (Sommerville), *R. austrinum.*—Fragrant bright gold, large trusses, vigorous to 8 feet, S, April, zone 6.

'Escatawpa' (Dodd), *R. austrinum.*—Fragrant bright gold, light red tubes, vigorous to 12 feet, CW, April, zone 6.

'Fall Fling' (Waldman/Roslyn), *R. arborescens* × *R. prunifolium.*—Red, 8 feet, S, September, zone 5.

'Fragrant Star' (Briggs).—Tetraploid conversion of 'Snowbird', similar to but larger in all parts, 5 feet, TC, April, zone 5.

'Framingham' (Mezitt/Weston), *R. viscosum* ×.—Deep pink in bud, opening to yellowish pink with yellow blotch, glaucous dark green foliage, 4 feet, S, July, zone 5.

'Frosty' (Towe-Anastos/Lazy K), same as 'Terry Greer', *R. alabamense.*—Fragrant white with yellow blotch, dark green foliage, 8 feet, CW, April, zone 6.

'Gable's Yellow' (Gable), *R. arborescens* × *R. cumberlandense.*—Moderately fragrant light yellow, semiglossy foliage, slow growth habit, 4 feet, CW, May, zone 5.

'Galle's Choice' (Galle), *R. alabamense* × *R. calendulaceum.*—Mildly fragrant medium yellow, white throat, wavy petal margins, 6 feet, S, May, zone 5.

'Gamecock' (Towe-Anastos/Lazy K), *R. calendulaceum* × *R. periclymenoides.*—Orange feather-petals age to red, floriferous, 4 feet, CW, April–May, zone 5.

'Georgia Belle' (Towe-Anastos/Lazy K), *R. arborescens* (var. *georgiana*).—Fragrant white, red pistils and filaments, dark green foliage, 6 feet, S, August, zone 5.

'Goldbrick' (Towe-Anastos/Lazy K), *R. arborescens* × *R. cumberlandense.*—Bright gold with darker gold blotch, red petioles, pistils, and filaments, compact to 4 feet, CW, May, zone 5.

'Golden Showers' (Mezitt/Weston), *R. prunifolium* × *R. viscosum.*—Fragrant peach, yellow, and white tricolor, narrow foliage, 5 feet, S, July, zone 5.

'Harry's Honey' (Beasley/Transplant), *R. flammeum.*—Orange, semiglossy foliage, stoloniferous to 5 feet, CW, April, zone 6.

'Independence' (Mezitt/Weston), *R. prunifolium* × *R. viscosum.*—Fragrant pink with long tubes, 5 feet, S, July, zone 5.

'Janet Jenkins' (Jenkins/Lazy K), *R. calendulaceum* × *R. canescens.*—Light pink ages to bright pink, orange blotch, compact to 5 feet, CW, April–May, zone 5.

'July Jester' (Leach), *R. cumberlandense* × *R. prunifolium.*—Orange-red with orange blotch, semiglossy foliage, 5 feet, S, July, zone 5.

'July Joy' (Leach), *R. cumberlandense* × *R. prunifolium.*—Salmon red with gold blotch, red tubes, compact growth habit, 5 feet, S, July, zone 5.

'Katie Ferguson' (Dodd), *R. viscosum* (var. *oblongifolium*).—Fragrant bright pink, twisted foliage, upright to 6 feet, CW, May, zone 5.

'Kelsey's Flame' (Beasley/Transplant), *R. calendulaceum.*—Orange-and-yellow bicolor, 6 feet, CW, May, zone 5.

'Keowee Sunset' (Towe-Anastos/Lazy K), *R. calendulaceum* × *R. periclymenoides.*—Large pink with solid gold upper petal, red tubes, pistils, and filaments, 6 feet, CW, April–May, zone 5.

'Lady Barbara' (Cummins), *R. arborescens* × *R. cumberlandense.*—Fragrant pink, glossy foliage, 6 feet, S, June, zone 5.

'Late Date' (Towe-Anastos/Transplant), *R. arborescens* (var. *georgiana*) × *R. prunifolium.*—Fragrant white, red pistils, semiglossy foliage, 6 feet, S, August, zone 5.

'Late Lady' (Cummins), *R. arborescens* × *R. prunifolium.*—Fragrant dark pink, dark green foliage, 6 feet, S, July–August, zone 5.

'Lavender Girl' (Beasley/Transplant), *R. periclymenoides.*—Fragrant soft lavender, 6 feet, CW, April, zone 5.

'Lisa's Gold' (Beasley/Transplant), *R. austrinum.*—Fragrant bright gold, light red tubes, vigorous to 10 feet, CW, April, zone 6.

'Little Red Riding Hood' (Beasley/Transplant), *R. prunifolium.*—Red, dark green foliage, upright to 8 feet, CW, August, zone 5.

'Magic' (Mezitt/Weston), *R. arborescens* × *R. cumberlandense.*—Opens yellow, ages to dark orange creating a bicolor effect, compact to 4 feet, S, June, zone 5.

'Magic Pink' (Towe-Anastos/Lazy K), *R. calendulaceum* × *R. periclymenoides*.—Pale pink changes to dark red, dark green foliage, sterile triploid, 6 feet, CW, May, zone 5.

'Marie Hoffman' (Hoffman), reported to be a polyploid form of *R. prinophyllum* but appears to be *R. prinophyllum* × *R. japonicum*.—Large fragrant pink, orange blotches, upright growth habit, 6 feet, S, May, zone 4.

'Marydel' (Hill), *R. atlanticum* × *R. periclymenoides*.—Fragrant white with strawberry red tubes and petal ribs, glaucous gray-green foliage, spreading and vigorous, 5 feet, CW, May, zone 5.

'Memory of Fred Galle' (Kehr/Lazy K), *R. arborescens* (var. *georgiana*) × *R. prunifolium*.—Fragrant yellow-and-pink bicolor, gold blotch, 8 feet, S, August, zone 5.

'Millennium' (Mezitt/Weston), 'Weston's Parade' × 'Weston's Sparkler'.—Moderately fragrant beet red with pale orange blotch, very glaucous blue-green foliage, 5 feet, S, July, zone 5.

'Millie Mac' (McConnell), *R. austrinum* limb sport.—Unusual fragrant gold picotee flowers with ⅛-inch white margins, red tubes, strong basal shoots often revert to solid yellow flowers, 6 feet, CW, April, zone 6.

'Mountain Creek White' (Towe-Anastos/Lazy K), F_2 *R. viscosum* (var. *montanum*) × 'Late Date'.—Fragrant white, wide pointed petals, thin tubes, floriferous, glossy dark green foliage, 5 feet, S, June, zone 5.

'My Mary' (Beasley/Transplant), *R. austrinum* × (*R. atlanticum* × *R. periclymenoides*).—Fragrant yellow, red tubes, thick dark green leaves, 6 feet, S, April, zone 5.

'Nacoochee Princess' (Beasley/Transplant), *R. atlanticum* × *R. periclymenoides*.—Fragrant white with pale pink overtones, pale yellow blotch, 6 feet, S, April, zone 5.

'Nancy Callaway' (Koone/Lazy K), *R. alabamense*.—Fragrant yellow-blotched white, dark glossy foliage, low spreading growth habit to 4 feet, CW, April, zone 6.

'Nectar' (Mezitt/Weston), *R. arborescens* × *R. cumberlandense*.—Red buds open to light pink inside with orange blotch and orange overtones, moderately fragrant, upright narrow foliage, slow growing, 4 feet, S, June–July, zone 5.

'Olde Gold' (Koone/Lazy K), *R. austrinum*.—Fragrant dark yellow with orange overtones, vigorous, 8 feet, S, April, zone 6.

'Orange Carpet' (Sommerville), *R. calendulaceum* × *R. flammeum*.—Bright orange, floriferous, low spreading growth habit to 2 feet high × 10 feet wide in fifteen years, CW, April, zone 5.

'Pastel #3' (McCartney/Woodlanders), *R. alabamense* × *R. canescens* × *R. flammeum* complex.—Fragrant light yellow, 6 feet, CW, April, zone 6.

'Pastel #4' (McCartney/Woodlanders), *R. alabamense* × *R. canescens* × *R. flammeum* complex.—Deep orange-red, 6 feet, CW, April, zone 6.

'Pastel #5' (McCartney/Woodlanders), *R. alabamense* × *R. canescens* × *R. flammeum* complex.—Bright yellow, 6 feet, CW, April, zone 6.

'Pastel #6' (McCartney/Woodlanders), *R. alabamense* × *R. canescens* × *R. flammeum* complex.—Bright orange, vigorous, 6 feet, S, April, zone 6.

'Pastel #7' (McCartney/Woodlanders), *R. alabamense* × *R. canescens* × *R. flammeum* complex.—Deep peach, 6 feet, CW, April, zone 6.

'Pastel #9' (McCartney/Woodlanders), *R. alabamense* × *R. canescens* × *R. flammeum* complex.—Deep orange, 6 feet, CW, April, zone 6.

'Pastel #10' (McCartney/Woodlanders), *R. alabamense* × *R. canescens* × *R. flammeum* complex.—Fragrant white with yellow blotch, 6 feet, CW, April, zone 6.

'Pastel #12 (McCartney/Woodlanders), *R. alabamense* × *R. canescens* × *R. flammeum* complex.—Dark peachy orange, 6 feet, CW, April, zone 6.

'Pastel #16' (McCartney/Woodlanders), *R. alabamense* × *R. canescens* × *R. flammeum* complex.—Fragrant white with yellow blotch, 6 feet, CW, April, zone 6.

'Pastel #18' (McCartney/Woodlanders), *R. alabamense* × *R. canescens* × *R. flammeum* complex.—Fragrant cream with yellow blotch, 6 feet, CW, April, zone 6.

'Pastel #20' (McCartney/Woodlanders), *R. alabamense* × *R. canescens* × *R. flammeum* complex.—Pink with orange overtones, 6 feet, CW, April, zone 6.

'Pastel #23' (McCartney/Woodlanders), *R. alabamense* × *R. canescens* × *R. flammeum* complex.—Fragrant pink, white, and yellow tricolor with white and yellow blotch, 6 feet, CW, April, zone 6.

'Pennsylvania' (Mezitt/Weston), *R. viscosum* × *R. prunifolium.*—Fragrant medium pink with orange blotch, upright growth habit, 5 feet, S, late August, zone 5.

'Phlox Pink' (Varnadoe), *R. canescens.*—Fragrant medium pink with violet tubes, dark green leaves, open upright growth habit with narrow base, 6 feet, S, April, zone 6.

'Pink Mist' (Johnson/Summer Hill), *R. viscosum.*—Fragrant light pink buds open to white flowers, upright habit to 6 feet, CW, May, zone 5.

'Pink Puff' (Leach), *R. arborescens* × *R. cumberlandense.*—Pink with yellow overtones, yellow blotch, glossy foliage, 5 feet, CW, June, zone 5.

'Pink Satin' (Koone/Lazy K), *R. arborescens* (var. *georgiana*) × *R. prunifolium.*—Mildly fragrant soft pink with yellow blotch, semiglossy foliage, 5 feet, S, July, zone 5.

'Pink & Sweet' (Mezitt/Weston), *R. arborescens* × *R. prunifolium.*—Fragrant purplish pink with white and yellow blotch, glossy convex foliage, compact to 4 feet, S, June, zone 5.

'Popcorn' (Mezitt/Weston), *R. arborescens* × *R. viscosum.*—Fragrant yellow-blotched white, pink pistils and stamens, glossy leaves glaucous underneath, 5 feet, S, June, zone 5.

'Popsicle' (Mezitt/Weston), *R. viscosum* × *R. cumberlandense.*—Fragrant dark pink, orange blotch, dark green foliage, 5 feet, S, June, zone 5.

'Purple' (McCartney/Woodlanders), same as 'Flat Creek Fuchsia', *R. periclymenoides.*—Fragrant pinkish purple with red tubes, semiglossy foliage, stoloniferous, compact to 4 feet, CW, May, zone 5.

'Purple Paladin' (Towe-Anastos/Roslyn), *R. periclymenoides.*—Fragrant medium purple with red tubes, compact to 5 feet, CW, May, zone 5.

'Quiet Thoughts' (Mezitt/Weston), *R. arborescens* × *R. cumberlandense*.—Fragrant yellow-and-orange bicolor, upright growth habit, 5 feet, S, May–June, zone 5.

'Random Red' (Towe-Anastos/Lazy K), *R. calendulaceum* × *R. periclymenoides*.—Variably orange-red to red, very red some years, glossy foliage, vigorous, 8 feet, CW, April–May, zone 5.

'Razzberry' (Sommerville), *R. canescens* × *R. flammeum*.—Bright raspberry red with yellow blotches, small leaves, compact to 4 feet, CW, April, zone 6.

'Rebel Yell' (Towe-Anastos/Roslyn), *R. prunifolium*.—Red, floriferous, tightly stoloniferous growth habit to 6 feet, CW, August, zone 5.

'Red Inferno' (Koone/Lazy K), *R. flammeum*.—Dark orange with yellow blotch, ages to vivid red, semiglossy foliage, vigorous growth habit, 6 feet, CW, April, zone 6.

'Red Ripple' (Towe-Anastos/Roslyn), *R. cumberlandense*.—Red, glossy rippled foliage, compact to 4 feet, CW, June, zone 5.

'Red Salute' (Mezitt/Weston), *R. prunifolium* × *R. viscosum*.—Fragrant cherry pink, tubular flowers, 4 feet, S, July, zone 5.

'Ribbon Candy' (Mezitt/Weston), *R. arborescens* × *R. cumberlandense*—Fragrant pink with white stripes, dark green foliage, 5 feet, S, June–July, zone 5.

'Riefler's White' (Riefler/Lazy K), *R. austrinum* limb sport.—Fragrant white with yellow blotch, red pistils, white filaments, basal shoots often revert to yellow, 6 feet, CW, April, zone 6.

'Rosy Cheeks' (Beasley/Transplant), *R. atlanticum* × *R. periclymenoides*.—Fragrant soft rose, gold blotch, convex blue-green foliage, dense, compact to 5 feet, S, May, zone 6.

'Sandy' (Mezitt/Weston), *R. arborescens* × *R. cumberlandense*.—Pink-and-yellow blend with strong yellow orange blotch, leaf margins upcurved, 3 feet, S, June, zone 5.

'Scarlet Salute' (Leach), *R. cumberlandense*.—Red, orange-red blotch, semiglossy foliage, 5 feet, S, June, zone 5.

'S. D. Coleman' (Leach), *R. prunifolium.*—Orange-red, spreading habit to 6 feet, S, August, zone 5.

'Sizzler' (Hill), *R. cumberlandense.*—Orange-red with yellow and pink overtones, slow growth to 5 feet, S, June, zone 5.

'Snowbird' (Biltmore Estate), *R. atlanticum* × *R. canescens.*—Very fragrant white, glaucous gray-green foliage, compact to 5 feet, CW, May, zone 5.

'Sparkler' (Mezitt/Weston), *R. viscosum* × *R. prunifolium.*—Fragrant ruffled pink, glaucous blue-green foliage, 5 feet, S, July, zone 5.

'Spring Pink' (Towe-Anastos/Lazy K), *R. canescens* × *R. flammeum.*—Fragrant dark pink, no blotch, starlike flowers have pointed petals, upright, 6 feet, CW, April, zone 6.

'Spring Rainbow' (Towe-Anastos/Lazy K), *R. calendulaceum* × *R. periclymenoides.*—Pale pink flowers age to medium pink then to dark pink, yellow blotches age to orange, red tubes, all colors show together, 6 feet, CW, May, zone 5.

'Summer Eyelet' (Beasley/Transplant), *R. viscosum.*—Mildly fragrant white, narrow reflexed petals, glossy dark green foliage, compact growth habit, 5 feet, CW, June, zone 5.

'Summer Lyric' (Beasley/Transplant), *R. arborescens* (var. *georgiana*) × *R. prunifolium.*—Fragrant pink, yellow blotch, 5 feet, S, July, zone 5.

'Sundance Yellow' (Towe-Anastos/RareFind), *R. calendulaceum* × *R. periclymenoides.*—Yellow, darker yellow blotch, light green foliage, compact growth habit, 4 feet, CW, April, zone 5.

'Sunlight' (Hill), *R. cumberlandense* with some *R. arborescens* influence.—Rose-red with orange overtones, yellow-orange blotch, dark green foliage, 5 feet, S, June, zone 5.

'Sweet September' (Cross), *R. arborescens* × *R. prunifolium.*—Mildly fragrant medium pink, dark green foliage, upright habit to 8 feet, S, September, zone 5.

'Tangelo' (Towe-Anastos/Summer Hill), *R. calendulaceum.*—Large orange, pale pink overtones some years, tight trusses, upright spreading growth habit to 6 feet, CW, May, zone 5.

'Timberline' (Towe-Anastos/Lazy K), *R. vaseyi.*—Dark pink with burgundy spots on upper petal, slightly compact growth habit, 5 feet, CW, May, zone 4.

'Toy' (Holsomback), *R. arborescens* × *R. viscosum.*—Fragrant light pink, glaucous blue-green foliage, 5 feet, S, June, zone 5.

'Wayah Crest' (Towe-Anastos/RareFind), *R. arborescens* × *R. cumberlandense.*—Moderately fragrant pinkish violet, small orange blotch, dark green foliage, 6 feet, CW, June, zone 5.

'Weston's Firecracker' (Mezitt/Weston), *R. viscosum* × *R. prunifolium.*—Mildly fragrant light red, dark green foliage, 5 feet, S, July, zone 5.

'Weston's Garden Party' (Mezitt/Weston), *R. arborescens* × *R. cumberlandense* × *R. viscosum.*—Deep pink, orange blotch, white petal ribs, 5 feet, S, July, zone 5.

'Weston's Innocence' (Mezitt/Weston), *R. arborescens* × *R. viscosum.*—Fragrant white with pale yellow blotch, vigorous but compact, 5 feet, S, June, zone 5.

'Weston's Lemon Drop' (Mezitt/Weston), *R. viscosum* ×.—Fragrant light yellow, vigorous, upright growth habit, 5 feet, S, July, zone 5.

'Weston's Lollipop' (Mezitt/Weston), *R. arborescens* × (*R. cumberlandense* × *R. viscosum*).—Pink, yellow blotch, 5 feet, S, June, zone 5.

'Weston's Parade' (Mezitt/Weston), *R. arborescens* × *R. prunifolium.*—Fragrant dark pink with orange blotch, upright growth habit, 5 feet, S, July, zone 5.

'Weston's Sparkler' (Mezitt/Weston), *R. arborescens* × *R. prunifolium.*—Fragrant ruffled dark pink flowers, glaucous blue-green foliage white underneath, 5 feet, S, July, zone 5.

'White Find' (LaBar), *R. vaseyi.*—Rare white selection with green spots on upper petal, vigorous, typical in other respects, 5 feet, CW, May, zone 4.

'White Foam' (Koone/Lazy K), *R. viscosum.*—Fragrant white, very floriferous, glaucous blue-green foliage, compact and dense to 3 feet, CW, June, zone 5.

'White Lightning' (Towe-Anastos/Transplant), *R. arborescens.*—Fragrant gold-blotched white, large flowers, dense and compact to 3 feet, CW, June, zone 5.

'White Pearl' (Koone/Lazy K), *R. viscosum* (var. *serrulatum*).—Fragrant white, dark green foliage, vigorous to 10 feet, CW, July–August, zone 6.

'Wise Decision' (Cummins), *R. austrinum.*—Fragrant golden yellow with wavy petal margins, light red tubes, vigorous to 8 feet, S, April, zone 6.

'Wood Nymph' (Beasley/Transplant), *R. flammeum.*—Vivid orange, large trusses, 6 feet, CW, April, zone 6.

'Yellow Delight' (Beasley/Transplant), *R. atlanticum* × *R. austrinum.*—Fragrant large soft yellow, light red tubes, vigorous, 5 feet, S, April, zone 6.

'Yohah' (Beasley/Transplant), *R. cumberlandense.*—Bright orange-red, reflexed petal tips, upright to 5 feet, CW, June, zone 5.

Chapter 8

Improving Azaleas: Future Possibilities

As successful as past and present breeding programs have been, improvements were made to very few of the many traits that can be found in azaleas. In reviewing the progress made thus far, especially in the Exbury, Ilam, and Knap Hill azaleas, the results are good indicators that more changes are possible. Flower size was increased from 1.5 inches to more than 3 inches in some instances. Cell ploidy was increased, as evidenced by thick-walled flowers, leathery leaves, and heavy wood. Flower pigment saturation was increased to produce colorfast flowers in a wide range of colors. Flowers with large yellow or orange blotches were developed, and double flowers were pushed to the limits of up to fifty petals per flower.

Recent breeding programs in the United States have led to late-blooming azaleas, cold-hardy azaleas, and early-blooming, heat-tolerant azaleas with large flowers. All of these efforts increased the popularity of azaleas and demonstrate that azaleas traits are relatively easy to manipulate. One of the problems preventing further improvements is a practical way to make unusual plants available to breeders. Azaleas with atypical traits, such as picotee flowers or flowers with feather-petals, are currently being propagated in an effort to give plant breeders access to plants to use to improve the traits. Other traits, such as azaleas with low, compact growth habits, are valuable for breeding. Few have been found, however, and most have proven difficult to propagate. In time perhaps plants with these traits will find their way into the hands of breeders who can take the necessary steps to bring new azaleas closer to our front doors.

Trait Inheritance

Understanding a few basic principles of genetics, transferring genetic knowledge from related genera, and using a measure of common sense will allow an azalea breeder to proceed with assurance that positive results can be achieved in a reasonable length of time. Genes, the basic units of heredity, are found in all plant cells and are arranged in strands called chromosomes. In 1866 Gregor Mendel, an Austrian monk and botanist, published research in which he identified two types of genes in sweet peas—dominant and recessive. Since then several other types of plant genes have been identified. Traits under the control of single dominant or recessive genes provide us with interesting and valuable breeding opportunities, especially in improving unusual flower types. If plants expressing these traits are bred correctly, some traits will reappear in F_1 (filial one or first generation) or F_2 seedlings in predictable ratios. For example, when a plant expressing a trait controlled by a single dominant gene is crossed with a plant lacking the trait (Aa × aa), half the F_1 seedlings will express the trait (Aa). When a plant expressing a trait controlled by a single recessive gene is crossed with a plant lacking the trait (aa × AA), all F_1 seedlings will be normal (Aa). However, if one of the F_1 seedlings is backcrossed to the parent with the atypical trait (Aa × aa), half of the F_2 seedlings will express the trait (aa), or if two of the F_1 siblings (sister seedlings) are crossed with each other (Aa × Aa), one-quarter of their progeny will express the trait.

Dick Jaynes found that the feather-petal trait (polypetala) in mountain laurels is under the control of a single recessive gene. Phil Waldman, owner of Roslyn Nursery on Long Island, however, found that not to be the case in evergreen azaleas. He crossed 'Koromo shikibu', which has feather-petal flowers, with 'Mt. Seven Star', which has normal flowers, and half the F_1 seedlings had the strap-petal trait, the expected 1:1 ratio for a trait under the control of a single dominant gene. These two examples show that a trait in closely related genera can vary in genetic control. There is evidence that several other traits in azaleas are under the control of user-friendly single dominant genes.

Many other traits are under polygenic (multiple-gene) control. Unlike single-gene traits that are either present or absent, these traits, even when present in only one parent, usually show up in varying degrees of intensity in F_1 seedlings. When both parents express the trait, almost all seedlings will express the trait and a few in a more pronounced manner than either parent. It is important to note that the mere presence of an unusual trait does not necessarily mean that it has breeding potential. Although determining the inheritance of any trait is a worthwhile goal from a research standpoint, some traits have limited horticultural value.

Reciprocal crosses.—When a cross is made to understand the genetics of a trait or to improve the trait, ideally a reciprocal cross should also be made. If pollen from plant A is placed onto plant B, the seeds that are later collected from plant B should be grown separately from those made by placing pollen from plant B onto plant A, which is referred to as the reciprocal cross. In many instances this is not possible due to the unavailability of pollen from one of the parents, as in some of the double-flowered types. Because some traits may be maternal—carried in the ovaries and not in the pollen—reciprocal crosses are a way to further sort out the genetic interactions that produce unusual traits.

Seedling numbers.—When growing seedlings from a cross, numerous recommendations have been made as to how many seedlings should be grown to insure the desired results are obtained. If color alone is the goal, about thirty seedlings from a yellow × yellow cross should reveal the general range of colors obtainable from that particular cross. In crosses in which two or more atypical traits are being combined, a few hundred seedlings may be needed to accurately reveal the complexity of the cross. The best rule is to grow as many seedlings as time and space permits.

Areas of Interest

It is often said that the devil is in the details, and this is especially true in plant breeding. Although the details can indeed be tedious, it is there that we find the genes for change. Flower shapes and types are rich in genetic potential. Foliage color and textures present an important group of subtle polygenic traits that can make fundamental changes in the way we view azaleas. Finally, growth habits present a few but important traits that have profound implications for change. Why these traits were not addressed in the past was probably due to the obvious interest in improving flower color and size and lack of access to plants with unusual flower types, foliage types, and growth habits. Also, in many instances it is only when a unique trait presents itself in a conspicuous manner that the bulb clicks on and its potential is realized. To those of us who are a bit slow on the uptake, this may have to happen several times before the moment of interocular impact—when something hits you right between the eyes—finally occurs. It should be noted that the ideas presented here also have applicability to ongoing breeding programs in which the focus is on heat-tolerant azaleas with large flowers or hardy azaleas, such as the Northern Lights Series.

IMPROVING FLOWERS

As uniform as azalea flowers may seem to be, there is considerable variation in fragrance, flower size, petal shape and thickness, and tube diameter and length. There is also wide variation in flower color, both in the wild and in cultivated hybrids. Although flower size and color have been exploited to reasonable limits, there are many other ways in which flowers can be improved.

Fragrance.—Smell has the strongest memory-inducing quality of our five senses. For some people fragrances can cause brief mental flashbacks to earlier places and times, and fragrant azaleas are no exception. Breeding for fragrance, which appears to be a polygenic trait, can be done if only one parent is fragrant. First generation seedlings from a fragrant × non-fragrant cross range from nonfragrant to mildly fragrant, whereas a fragrant × fragrant cross usually produces all fragrant progeny. This trait may also be tied to color, as fragrant red and red-purple flowers are rare. Because fragrance is found in several species and is a desirable quality, including the trait in any cross should be given due consideration.

Color changes.—As noted earlier, azaleas frequently undergo color changes throughout the season. These can be especially interesting if the change is from light to dark. Several such selections can be found in the cultivar list and, because the trait is probably polygenic, crosses between two of them should be worthwhile. Some cultivars notable for their changes are 'Dawn at the River', 'Doctor Helen', 'Magic Pink' (possibly sterile), and 'Spring Rainbow'.

A new color.—Several years ago Britt Smith and Frank Mossman decided to "create" a yellow *Rhododendron occidentale*, a color not found in that species. They had heard that a western azalea with yellow flowers had been found but were unable to get information on its location. They had found plants with yellow pigment in the blotch area, as well as on some of the petals, so they decided to start with the best of these. The two best plants were crossed, the two best near-yellow F_1 seedlings were crossed and, as they expected, several F_2 seedlings were very yellow (a photograph appears in the plate section). This simple experiment illustrates how a new color was created in an azalea species lacking yellow flowers.

The primary colors in species azaleas are white, yellow, orange, light red (pink), and red, and flowers with yellow or orange blotches are also common. Additionally, salmon (a wide range of colors between yellow or orange and pink or rose) flowers are common in the wild and are easy to produce from appropriate crosses. Likewise, red-purple flowers, commonly referred to as dark pink or rose, may also arise when a white or pink azalea is crossed with an orange or red azalea.

Blue pigment is frequently visible in dry flowers, and there is evidence that flowers can be developed that move us a few steps closer to that color. This is not to say that blue azaleas are possible, or desirable, but purple flowers, similar in color to purple cabbages, are probably within the realm of possibility. Blue pigment is most commonly seen in some of the more richly colored forms of *R. periclymenoides* and *R. calendulaceum* × *R. periclymenoides* hybrids. A breeding program to pursue purple flowers should produce interesting results.

Flower shapes.—One weakness of some azaleas is flowers with narrow petals or that are made narrow by back-folded margins. These flowers can be found in all species but are more common in the white and pink species. *Rhododendron viscosum* is notorious for having narrow petals, as are *R. periclymenoides* and *R. canescens*. The nonfragrant orange to red species can have very wide, flat petals. Wide petals give a flower a more substantial look, regardless of whether the petal tip is pointed or rounded. In one instance a compact *R. viscosum* with glossy foliage, thin tubes, and narrow petals was crossed with an *R. arborescens* × *R. prunifolium* hybrid with glossy foliage and flowers with wide petals. Most of the seedlings had glossy foliage, and some had the thin tubes of *R. viscosum*. One seedling,

'Mountain Creek White', combined the traits of dark, glossy foliage, thin tubes, well-shaped petals with crisp margins, and red petioles. This shows that several foliage and flower traits can be combined in one generation.

In contrast to petals with smooth margins, some have ruffled margins, a trait that gives flowers a more three-dimensional look. This is a valuable trait that should be easy to improve by crossing two plants with the trait. Like other unusual floral traits, ruffled margins seem to be more common in hybrids than in species and are often seen in *Rhododendron calendulaceum* and its hybrids.

Flower types.—If examined closely in the wild, azaleas express a wide range of flower types that have considerable potential for improvement. Most of these traits are probably under the control of a single gene, but in some instances it is not known whether the traits are dominant or recessive. If we are to fully exploit the genetic potential of azaleas, these questions need to be answered.

The apetala trait is fairly rare in azaleas and results from the five petals being replaced by five extra stamens. In some areas these flowers are referred to as "cat-whiskers," a term not entirely without merit. A flower consists of a pistil and ten stamens, making it look somewhat like a small artist's brush. The trait is variable, and in some instances a few of the filaments are flattened into narrow petals. The trait seems to have little value other than to the hard-core collector and in understanding its genetic control. It is doubtful the trait could be improved to the point that it would have widespread appeal.

Of the several flower types in azaleas, the polypetala trait is one of the most attractive. In this type the petals are split to the calyx and each petal falls separately. In some expressions the petals are short or narrow, or both, whereas in others the petals have good substance and are wide near the tips with narrow bases. 'Gamecock', a hardy hybrid that is available commercially, is a good expression of the trait. Crossing it with a fragrant white or pink selection with glossy, dark foliage could lead to improvements in flowers and foliage. The polypetala trait is under the control of a single dominant gene in evergreen azaleas.

Some azaleas occasionally have flowers with extra petals. In this type the extra petals are due to some of the sepals of the calyx morphing into petals. These extra petals, usually two or three per flower, merge between the five normal petals. Because a calyx has five sepals, there is the potential to develop flowers with ten petals instead of five, which would give them a more rounded look.

Under normal circumstances an azalea flower has five petals with the upper petal being somewhat wider and more symmetrical along its linear axis than the four side petals. Several flower types fall into the double category, with the following having been observed, although there are probably more expressions of the trait:

semidouble: five petals with partially petalloid filaments;
double: five petals with five fully petalloid filaments;
full double: five petals and numerous petalloid filaments;
hose-in-hose: two corollas, usually with five normal filaments;
semidouble hose-in-hose: two corollas and some petalloid filaments;
double hose-in-hose: two corollas and five fully petalloid filaments; and
full double hose-in-hose: two corollas with numerous petalloid filaments.

In Ilam azaleas, breeders have developed flowers with up to fifty petals. It should be easy to duplicate these efforts and produce stable flowers of any of the double types. Denis Hughes of New Zealand crossed a double Ghent azalea with an Ilam azalea with single flowers. Of the 300 seedlings he grew from the cross, 160 had double flowers, very close to the expected 1:1 ratio for a trait controlled by a single dominant gene. This suggests that other double traits may be under the control of a single gene.

Azaleas with picotee flowers fall into two categories. Typical picotee flowers have darker petal margins, and the trait is probably polygenic. 'Millie Mac', a second type, was found as a limb sport on a *Rhododendron austrinum*, though its red tubes suggest it may have some *R. canescens* in its family tree. The yellow flowers of 'Millie Mac' make an abrupt change to ⅛-inch white margins, a hint the trait may be controlled by a single gene. To improve hardiness, margin width, and flower size, 'Millie Mac' should be crossed with a large-flowered hardy orange or red azalea. If F_1 seedlings lack the trait, two of the best seedlings should be crossed with each other. If the trait segregates in F_2 seedlings, selections should be made for flower size, margin width, and overall thriftiness. 'Millie Mac' is available commercially from several sources.

IMPROVING FOLIAGE

After producing flowers for ten days, give or take a few days, we are left with the foliage of an azalea to contemplate until the leaves drop in autumn. It is at this point that azaleas fade into the background, both literally and figuratively, until next year. As a group azaleas have rather ho-hum foliage and unremarkable growth habits. Some azaleas, however, stir the imagination as to how improvements in foliage traits could make azaleas shrubs for all seasons. While some of these polygenic traits are subtle, they are no less important than flower color or type.

Leaf shape.—Azalea foliage falls within three shapes, and no one shape is intrinsically more attractive than the other. Elliptical leaves are widest in the center and taper toward either end. Obovate leaves, perhaps the most common, are widest near the tips. Orbicular leaves are nearly round. Azaleas seldom have ovate foliage, which is widest near the base. If examined closely, a limb will usually display a range of leaf shapes, with the leaves nearest the tip of the limb being the narrowest. A typical leaf for a given azalea will usually be found about half way from the first to the last leaf on a limb. Azaleas with unusually wide or narrow leaves can be attractive, and leaf shape is easy to manipulate through crosses between azaleas with leaves of similar shapes.

Leaf color.—Azalea leaves vary in color from yellow-green to medium green to dark green. Some leaves are also covered with a waxy powder that gives them distinct gray or blue overtones. The undersides of the leaves may be light gray or nearly white. In the wild, azaleas with dark green leaves or dark blue-green leaves with white undersides are very showy, and the traits set those plants apart, regardless of flower color. 'Millennium', one of the newest Weston introductions, has mildly fragrant red flowers—an unusual combination—and glaucous, blue-green leaves. Other selections with blue-green leaves include 'Delaware Blue', 'Rosy Cheeks', and 'Toy'.

In the spring of 2002 Ernest Koone, owner of Lazy K Nursery, spotted a *Rhododendron canescens* with red leaves in a block of seedlings and set it aside for evaluation. New leaf color is very showy, similar to Japanese maple 'Bloodgood', and is probably due to excessive anthocyanin pigment. Later in the season the color changes to dark green, but secondary flushes of growth that appear after the initial flush are also red. The fragrant white flowers are typical for the species. This interesting new plant adds another dimension to foliage traits.

Variegated leaves.—Reports of variegated foliage in the wild are increasing, indicating that some variegation may be pathogenic in nature. In some instances, however, it is stable. Because variegation is transmitted maternally, a variegated plant must be used as the seed parent in breeding for the trait. If some of the seedlings do not show variegation within a year from germination, the trait was probably viral in nature.

Petiole color.—The color of a leaf petiole is usually of little interest until a plant is found with bright or dark red petioles. Red petioles, which are more prominent during the spring, add interest to leaves up close, and the trait shows up in crosses in varying degrees when only one parent has the trait. Red petioles are most often found in *Rhododendron arborescens* or *R. arborescens* × *R. cumberlandense* hybrids. 'Goldbrick' and 'Mountain Creek White' have red petioles.

Leaf texture.—Most azaleas have leaves with slightly raspy surfaces, caused by short, stiff hairs. Some species, however, such as *Rhododendron arborescens*, have leaves with smooth, glossy surfaces. Some azaleas also have leaves with distinct lateral veins, giving the leaves a ribbed, corrugated appearance. Leaves can also have margins that are slightly downturned, which makes them look thicker than they actually are. These traits can be found in individual plants in all species but are more common in hybrids and *R. viscosum*.

GROWTH HABITS

To give azaleas an entirely new look, improving foliage is secondary to improving growth habits. Unfortunately, plants with the potential to do so are few and far between. Because most gardeners are interested in flowers first, and perhaps foliage as an afterthought, developing azaleas with atypical growth habits may be the last frontier to be conquered. The few azaleas that have been found with atypical growth habits indicate there are probably other types yet to be discovered.

Compact azaleas.—Several compact azaleas have been found, but unfortunately few have been propagated. One of the best resides in the garden of Earl and Verdie Sommerville of Marietta, Georgia. It is a *Rhododendron arborescens × R. cumberlandense × R. viscosum* seedling that is 30 inches high and 40 inches wide. Its growth habit is attributable to heavy bud set, short shoots—about 3 inches per year—and multiple, wide-angle vegetative buds. The leaves are semiglossy, only slightly smaller than normal, and the orange-blotched pink flowers are fragrant. The plant is densely layered and looks like a compact evergreen azalea. Efforts are underway to propagate it, and it has been used in crosses, the results of which are not yet known.

Another source of compact azaleas is witches'-brooms, although they are rare on deciduous azaleas. A broom is a dense, congested mass of growth probably caused by leafhoppers. Brooms are common on evergreen azaleas, and when rooted the cuttings remain compact. In one instance a broom was found on a *Rhododendron canescens*. The flowers were normal in size but opened a few days before the flowers on the plant to which it was attached. The broom flowers were pollinated from a nearby normal plant and the seeds collected and germinated. Shortly after germination several of the seedlings showed compact growth habits, but in a few months they reverted to normal. This instability indicates the broom was caused by disease, although a stable one could easily lead to a line of compact azaleas, as has been done with some conifers.

Fastigiate azaleas.—As in plants of most genera, fastigiate (narrow and upright) azaleas are found in the wild or occasionally in seed-lots. The habit is caused in part by vegetative buds that lie at low angles to the previous year's growth. Ideally the height-to-width ratio should be about 3:1; if the plant is too narrow and dense, inner limbs can become diseased. Most fastigiate azaleas are compact and slow to set buds, and no breeding results have been reported on the trait.

Prostrate azaleas.—Azaleas with prostrate (flat) growth habits are rare and usually unstable. The trait may have value for developing azaleas that will cascade over walls or grow on trellises. Earl Sommerville's 'Orange Carpet' has a fairly flat growth habit with a mature width of about 10 feet with a 3-foot mound in the center. Self-pollinating the plant could produce similar seedlings that could be used to improve the trait.

Tree azaleas.—Occasionally tall azaleas, most frequently hybrids involving *Rhododendron calendulaceum*, are found that have from one to three trunks with most or all of the limbs near the tops. At first glance, they appear to be the remains of azaleas that lost some of their trunks to disease or falling trees. If the boles of these azaleas are examined closely, however, they lack the tell-tale scarring that should be present. Other traits suggest these azaleas may be genetically inclined to grow as small trees. Most have thick trunks, leaves that are larger and thicker than normal, and large flowers. Crosses between two such azaleas could easily answer the questions and could lead to azaleas that grow as small trees without pruning. The trait should show up in seedlings within two years after germination.

Combining Traits

Improving individual traits is a beginning to understanding azalea genetics, but the ultimate value of these traits will not be fully realized until they are combined in various ways. Large picotee flowers would certainly be attractive, but if that trait was combined with dark, glossy foliage and a compact growth habit, the results would be even more impressive. Combining some traits may prove easy, whereas combining others may take several generations to accomplish. The warning is that while changes can indeed be brought about, exposing the full complexity of azaleas will not come quickly. When traits are combined, however, there is the likelihood that other unimagined traits will appear, presenting further breeding opportunities. In breeding for single and combination traits, seedlings that do not express traits of interest should also be given appropriate evaluation based on their own merits.

Other Opportunities for Change

Without getting too abstract, there are other opportunities to make changes in azaleas. In most instances, however, they should be attempted by plant breeders who have the patience to make crosses that set few seeds, some of which may not germinate.

INDUCED POLYPLOIDY

An azalea is referred to as a haploid when it has 13 chromosomes (a rare condition), a diploid when it has 26 chromosomes, a triploid (usually sterile) when it has 39 chromosomes, a tetraploid when it has 52 chromosomes, and a hexaploid when it has 72 chromosomes. Because verifying ploidy requires laboratory work, the term *polyploid* is more appropriate for those unexamined plants that are suspected of having more than the normal complement of 26 chromosomes. Indicators of polyploidy are thick leathery leaves, dark green leaf color, larger and longerlasting flowers, compactness in some instances, and an increase in stem diameter.

Converting diploids plants to polyploids is a practice that is receiving more attention. During the micropropagation process a chemical, usually colchicine, is added to a culture in hopes of causing the plant to double its chromosomes. If successful, the conversion is grown on to maturity and evaluated to determine if it warrants being propagated commercially. In recent years Briggs Nursery introduced the elepidote rhododendron 'Tetra Nova', lepidote rhododendron 'Northern Starburst', and deciduous azaleas 'Western Lights' and 'Western Star', which were converted from 'Nova Zembla', 'PJM Compact', 'Orchid Lights', and 'Snowbird', respectively. Although these selections were converted to improve their horticultural value, some may have value for breeding purposes.

Crosses between plants at the polyploid level are frequently more successful than at the diploid level. Polyploid conversions of *Rhododendron vaseyi* and *R. schlippenbachii* might well cross with each other or with tetraploids *R. canadense* or *R. calendulaceum*. A polyploid conversion of *R. sanctum*, one of the deciduous azaleas of the *Tsutsutsi* subgenus, could open the door for *Pentathera* × *Tsutsutsi* hybrids or other wide crosses.

AZALEODENDRONS

Azaleodendrons result from crosses between azaleas and rhododendrons. In most instances they are produced by controlled crossed, but several wild *Rhododendron macrophyllum* × *R. occidentale* azaleodendrons have been verified. Most of those that have been propagated commercially are collectables with little value. Deciduous azaleas more readily cross with elepidote rhododendrons, and evergreen azaleas more readily cross with lepidote rhododendrons. Tetraploid *R. calendulaceum* and polyploid 'Western Star' × evergreen rhododendron 'Tetra Nova' are two crosses that could yield interesting results. In crosses such as these, the rhododendron should be used as the seed parent.

DECIDUOUS SECTION HYBRIDS

Four of the Northern Lights azaleas, including three new introductions, are *Pentathera* × *Rhodora* section hybrids between tetraploid *Rhododendron canadense* and diploid *R. japonicum* × *R. molle* seedlings. These crosses are difficult to make due to differences in the number of chromosomes and physiology. Because the crosses produced viable but sterile seedlings, renewed attempts should be made to cross *R. canadense* with *R. vaseyi* and with all members of section *Pentathera*, especially *R. calendulaceum*.

In some instances wide crosses have been successful when the stigmas were clipped from the flowers being pollinated. Stigmas have chemical and mechanical means to block foreign pollen, and by removing them and placing the pollen directly on the cut end of the style, fertilization may take place.

DECIDUOUS × EVERGREEN SUBGENUS HYBRIDS

The late August Kehr was a U.S. Department of Agriculture geneticist who retired in the 1970s and moved to North Carolina. He immediately began working on a yellow evergreen azalea by borrowing pigment genes from deciduous azaleas. After twenty-five years he failed to accomplish this, but what he learned along the way makes his goal very realistic today. He began by crossing several white diploid evergreen azaleas with an orange *Rhododendron calendulaceum*, but none of the crosses produced viable seeds. He then crossed several naturally tetraploid evergreen Satsuki azaleas ('Banka', 'Wako', 'Taihai', and 'Gettsu-toku') with *R. calendulaceum* and got a few viable seeds. The F_1 seedlings proved to be weak after germination, but some eventually regained normal vigor. At maturity they resembled evergreen azaleas and produced flowers a year earlier than deciduous azaleas. Their flowers were pinkish tan, suggesting the pink-flecked white Satsukis were carrying genes for pink pigment and that the orange *R. calendulaceum* did not carry as yellow, as hoped for. Kehr abandoned that line of breeding until he could find suitable parents.

Colchicine, a toxic crystalline substance extracted from bulbs of the autumn crocus, *Crocus autumnale*, has long been used to treat gout. If applied correctly to germinating azalea seeds, it has the ability to double their chromosome number. Using a method he developed, Kehr treated germinating white evergreen diploid seeds with colchicine and later selected several seedlings that he described as recessive for the color white and carrying no hidden genes for color. These azaleas have white flowers of heavy substance with thick, round, dark green leaves, and cross readily with *R. calendulaceum*. Unfortunately, failing health prevented him from germinating his last batch of seeds from these crosses.

Bright yellow forms of *Rhododendron calendulaceum* are fairly easy to locate, but other azaleas can be used to continue this work. Kehr suggested using a fragrant yellow Exbury azalea, hoping that both fragrance and pigment would transfer to F_1 seedlings. According to Kehr, the deciduous azalea must be used as the seed parent because yellow carotenoid pigments are not transmittable by pollen. He also recommended the tetraploid Satsukis be crossed again with a bright yellow polyploid deciduous azalea. He came to this conclusion after realizing the orange *R. calendulaceum* used in the first cross may have been the culprit that caused the pinkish tan flowers and not the pink-flecked Satsuki azaleas.

Chapter 9

Introducing New Azaleas

As an outdoor recreation—and despite the ups and downs of economic conditions—landscaping continues to grow in popularity. As gardeners become more knowledgeable, there is an increasing awareness of the invasive qualities of many common perennials, shrubs, and trees. This awareness has led to a new interest in indigenous American plants that have been in our back yards all along, including azaleas.

As new and improved azaleas are developed, a few will eventually find their way into the marketplace. Introducing azaleas into the wholesale and retail trade can be both a rewarding and frustrating experience. Before attempting to introduce a new azalea, a plant breeder or collector should be aware of several realities. In today's world of patented and trademarked plants, there might be some hope that a new azalea might lead to fame and fortune. If this is the expectation, the time will be better spent in some other venture. Another reality is that a truly exceptional azalea may never receive the recognition it deserves. Finally, it should be understood from the beginning that, as colorful as they are, azaleas will always be shrubs appreciated by relatively few gardeners.

Evaluating New Cultivars

The first pitfall to avoid in selecting a new azalea is ownership bias, a very subjective issue. There are ways, however, to minimize the bias so that a relatively objective determination can be made as to whether the azalea is industrial grade. A part of the process is to be intimately familiar with azaleas already in the trade, especially those that have similar characteristics. This familiarity may involve reading descriptions in catalogs, visiting gardens and observing plants for comparison, obtaining slides of cultivars from various sources or the Internet, or consulting someone who is familiar with them. For the azalea to be a viable product, ideally it should have at least one quality that sets it apart in a distinct and immediately recognizable way from other similar cultivars. These qualities might include a new color or color combination, superior foliage, an unusual growth habit, or unusual flowers. For example 'Gamecock', a feather-petal selection, may be the first of this type to be offered commercially, although it will eventually be pushed aside by improved feather-petal types.

New cultivars will come from two primary sources: plants found in the wild and seedlings grown from controlled crosses. A plant from either source should be thoroughly evaluated, though the methods will vary. When a unique selection is found in the wild, ideally the plant should be visited several times over a three-year period. If the plant is some distance away, this may present a problem. The azalea should be evaluated for hardiness, flower color, color stability, pest and disease resistance, foliage appearance, and overall thriftiness.

A plant grown from seeds in a container presents different evaluation challenges. A plant containerized since infancy and grown under nursery conditions receives daily watering and a steady trickle of fertilizer. This process produces a plant that is more vigorous, has thick wood and lustrous leaves, and may be more floriferous than it actually is when placed in the garden. Evaluating a prospective candidate in a container over a three-year period can lead to false conclusions. To avoid this dilemma, the azalea should be planted in the ground and grown and evaluated under typical garden conditions for at least two years. Under these conditions, many azaleas will lose the initial appeal they had and give the owner an opportunity to reevaluate.

Naming and Registering Cultivars

After a selection has passed the evaluation tests, selecting a cultivar name may be the next step. Due to the large number of azaleas that have been used over the years, this is not as easy as it sounds. Simple names that give some hints about the azalea are preferred. A plant's name can have an effect on how well the plant does from a commercial standpoint. The name 'Jack the Ripper' may turn customers away, whereas 'Red Sunset' may attract customers.

Another decision regarding the name of the plant is whether to register it with the American Rhododendron Society, which is monitored by the Royal Horticultural Society. (Appendix C reproduces azalea registration forms of the American Rhododendron Society.) The advantage of registration is that a historical record can be kept of the origin of the plant. The process is not difficult, but there are some American Rhododendron Society requirements that need to be taken into consideration, particularly in the areas of parentage and color descriptions. Registering an azalea with the American Rhododendron Society does not guarantee that the name will remain intact. There are many plants in the nursery trade being sold under more than one name, and to later learn that a favorite azalea has been renamed should come as no surprise. Although the practice is unethical, it is not illegal unless the plant is trademarked or patented. The bright side of the problem is that the plant is out there for others to enjoy, which should be the primary reason any plant is made available to the public.

RECORD-KEEPING

During the breeding process, accurate records should be kept of the parentage and date of each cross and the results obtained. Notations on parentage tell two things: the azaleas used in the cross and the sequence that was followed. When *Rhododendron viscosum* pollen is placed onto *R. flammeum*, the correct notation would be *R. flammeum* × *R. viscosum*. This follows the tradition of ladies first by indicating the seed or pod (female) parent to the left of the ×, the symbol used to indicate a cross. As further crosses are made, notations can become more complicated and require the use of parentheses and brackets. If a seedling from the above cross was later used to pollinate a plant of *R. prinophyllum*, the notation would be R. prinophyllum × (R. flammeum × R. viscosum). In the notation R. prino-phyllum × [(R. flammeum × R. viscosum) × (R. prunifolium × R. cumberlan-dense)], R. prunifolium was pollinated by R. cumberlandense in the initial cross. A seedling from that cross was later used to pollinate a R. flammeum × R. viscosum seedling, and finally a seedling from that cross was used to pollinate R. prinophyllum.

The parents of wild hybrids can be determined in some instances, but there is no way to know which species was the seed parent. In these cases the best rule to follow is alphabetical order, thus Rhododendron arborescens × R. cumberlandense can be used to denote an azalea having that parent-age. In a wild hybrid involving three species, no parentheses are used, and the notation R. arborescens × R. cumberlandense × R. viscosum is appropri-ate. Also the notation "collected in the wild" lets us know that the parent-age and crossing sequence is subject to question.

COLOR DESCRIPTIONS

For informal purposes, it is common to describe the color of an azalea by comparing it to a known object. This method, however, is not satisfac-tory in the more formal process of registering azaleas that may later be propagated for commercial release. An azalea said to be canary yellow does not give an accurate description of the color due to differences in perceptions as to what constitutes that color. Adjectives such as vivid, dark, pale, and light also fail to accurately describe colors. The RHS Col-our Chart, available from the Royal Horticultural Society, contains four sets of color fans that can be used to match flower color. Almost without exception, a numbered color swatch can be found to match any azalea color. Fan 1 has swatches of yellow, yellow-orange, orange-red, and red. One of the numerous colors that closely approximates canary yellow is Yellow Group 12. This alphanumeric system is not without flaws, but it is the best method available to accurately communicate flower color.

Commercial Propagation and Distribution

After an azalea has passed all initial tests, the owner is now faced with get-ting the cultivar into commercial production. Because rooting cuttings can be a slow process, a good approach is to develop a relationship with a micropropagation lab. Provided no major problems arise, a lab can begin to turn out large numbers of plants two years after it goes into culture. The small liners, from 1 to 3 inches tall, are then sold to wholesale and retail nurseries to grow until they are large enough to sell. In some instances liners can be pushed to bloom in two years. Labs differ in the material they use to propagate azaleas. Some require a containerized plant so a systemic fungicide can be applied to decrease the chances of contamination during the initial isolation process. Other labs work from dormant vegetative or floral buds taken from plants in the winter.

If cuttings are sent to a nursery for propagation, it should be noted from personal experience that repeatedly taking large quantities of cuttings, even from a vigorous plant, can damage it to the point of death. After a large quantity of cuttings has been taken, wait one or two years before taking cuttings again to allow the plant to regenerate. An alternative method is to take only a dozen or so cuttings each year until the nursery gets them rooted. The nursery can then take cuttings from the rooted cuttings, which in most instances will root easier than cuttings from the stock plant.

After a cultivar has been propagated in sufficient numbers, the small liners will be sold to wholesale and retail nurseries. The success of a new cultivar will depend on how easily and quickly it grows into a salable plant and how well it does in containers. Ultimately, the consumer will determine the fate of the plant. If it does not sell, for whatever reason, the plant will eventually fade into obscurity. This weeding-out process, however, is beneficial to the long-term popularity of azaleas.

A Final Note

For those of us who enjoy plants, we should try to keep a healthy perspective on our interest in them. Growing plants can be an entertaining facet of our lives, but one interest should not prevent us from exploring other avenues of growth. The fabric of life is full of many intertwined threads, and becoming self-actualized is best accomplished when we strive to weave as many threads into our lives as possible. As this book nears completion, the piles of material are fast disappearing from my desk. With some luck I will stumble onto another interest, but thoughts of azaleas will always be close at hand. At my age hiking the Appalachian Trail is out of the question, but basket weaving is a noble craft that may have some possibilities.

Appendix A

Azalea Organizations

American Rhododendron Society
11 Pinecrest Drive
Fortuna, California 95540
www.rhododendron.org

Azalea Society of America
1000 Moody Bridge Road
Cleveland, South Carolina 29635
www.azaleas.org

Rhododendron Species Botanical
   Garden
PO Box 3798
Federal Way, Washington 98063
www.rhodygarden.org

The Royal Horticultural Society
80 Vincent Square
London, SW1P 2PE
United Kingdom
www.rhs.org.uk

Appendix B

Azalea Sources

Broken Arrow Nursery
13 Broken Arrow Road
Hamden, Connecticut 06518
(203) 288-1026
www.brokenarrownursery.com
Dick Jaynes
mail order, retail

Carlson's Gardens
Box 305R
South Salem, New York 10590
(914) 763-5958
www.carlsonsgardens.com
Bob Carlson
mail order

Greer Gardens
1280 Goodpasture Road
Eugene, Oregon 97401
(800) 548-0111
www.greergardens.com
Harold Greer
mail order

Dodd & Dodd Wholesale Nursery
9585 Wulff Road South
Semmes, Alabama 36575
(334) 645-2222
Tommy Dodd
wholesale

Lazy K Nursery
705 Wright Road
Pine Mountain, Georgia 31822
(706) 663-4991
www.lazyknursery.com
Ernest Koone III
wholesale, retail, mail order

RareFind Nursery
957 Patterson Road
Jackson, New Jersey 08527
(732) 833-0613
Hank Schannen
mail order

Roslyn Nursery
211 Burrs Lane
Dix Hills, New York 11746
(631) 643-9347
www.roslynnursery.com
Phil Waldman
mail order

Stoneboro Nursery
88 Barbour Road
Stoneboro, Pennsylvania 16153
(814) 786-7991
Bill Barbour
wholesale micropropagated liners

Summer Hill Nursery
888 Summer Hill Road
Madison, Connecticut 06443
(203) 421-3055
Mike Johnson
wholesale

Transplant Nursery
1586 Parkertown Road
Lavonia, Georgia 30553
(706) 356-8947
Jeff and Lisa Beasley
wholesale

Wayside Gardens
1 Garden Lane
Hodges, South Carolina 29695
(800) 213-0379
www.waysidegardens.com
mail order

Weston Nurseries
East Main Street
Hopkinton, Massachusetts 01748
(508) 435-3414
www.westonnurseries.com
Wayne Mezitt
retail, wholesale

Whitney Gardens
PO Box 170
Brinnon, Washington 98320
(800) 952-2404
www.whitneygardens.com
mail order

Woodlanders
1128 Colleton Avenue
Aiken, South Carolina 29801
(803) 648-7522
www.woodlanders.net
Robert McCartney
mail order

Appendix C

Rhododendron Registration Forms

APPLICATION for REGISTRATION of a RHODODENDRON or AZALEA NAME

Send completed registration to: Jay W Murray, Registrar of Plant Names
21 Squire Terrace, Colts Neck, NJ 07722
Phone: 1-732-946-8627 e-mail: arsreg@yahoo.com

There is no fee for registration of a plant name. A selected clone of either a species or a hybrid may be named. Please refer to instruction sheet for guidance in preparing the application.

Please give name, phone & email of the person to whom the registrar may address questions:

Name _____ Phone _____ email_____

Proposed name of plant _____

Certificate requested   ☐ Yes or ☐ No

Has any other name been used for this plant ?   ☐ Yes or ☐ No

If Yes, give name_____

Identification number(s), if known: Collector No._____ ARS Seed Exch No. _____Breeder No._____

This is (check one): ☐ elepidote rhododendron;   ☐ lepidote rhododendron;   ☐ azaleodendron;

☐ deciduous azalea; ☐ evergreen azalea; ☐ vireya rhododendron; ☐ intergeneric hybrid

Complete Section A or Section B, whichever is applicable

SECTION A - SELECTED CLONE OF A SPECIES

Name of species, subspecies, variety, or form _____

Selected by (Name & Address)_____

_____ (Year) __ _____

SECTION B - SELECTED CLONE OF A HYBRID

Seed parent _____

Pollen parent _____

☐ Hybridized or   ☐ Selected by (Name & Adddress) _____

_____ (Year) _____

ALL APPLICANTS SHOULD COMPLETE Sections C and D

SECTION C - PLANT HISTORY

Grown to first flower by (Name & Address) _____

_____(Year) _____

Named by (Name & Address) _____

_____(Year) _____

Commercial introducer (Name & Address) _____

_____(Year) _____

Registered by (Name of person or firm & Address)_____

_____(Year) _____

Has the name been published with a description ? ☐ Yes or ☐ No   If so, when, where and by whom:

_____

Details of any awards or patents _____

SECTION D - DESCRIPTION   (Please refer to instruction sheet for illustrations)

Number of flowers per truss _____   Truss size: height _____ width _____

Truss shape: ☐ dome; ☐ ball; ☐ conical; ☐ flat; ☐ lax; ☐ other(specify) _____

Corolla shape (see instruction sheet) _____

Corolla: length _____ , width _____ , Number of lobes _____

Lobe margins: ☐ wavy; ☐ frilly; ☐ flat .   Scent: ☐ strong; ☐ moderate; ☐ slight; ☐ none.

Flower color: (a) buds_____

(b) inside flower _____
_____

(c) outside flower _____
_____

(d) color and distribution of blotch/spots _____

Note Color Chart used _____

Calyx length _____   Calyx color _____

Leaf: length _____, width _____, Margin: ☐ flat; ☐ wavy; ☐ upcurved; ☐ downcurved

Leaf shape: ☐ elliptic; ☐ lanceolate; ☐ ovate; ☐ obovate; ☐ oblong;

☐ orbicular; ☐ linear; ☐ other (specify) _____

Leaf base: ☐ cuneate; ☐ rounded; ☐ oblique; ☐ cordate; ☐ other (specify) _____

Leaf tip: ☐ acuminate; ☐ acute; ☐ broadly acute; ☐ obtuse; ☐ other (specify) _____

Leaf surface: ☐ dull; ☐ semi-glossy; ☐ glossy

Leaf color: _____

Indumentum type ☐ hairs; ☐ scales; ☐ none,

Indumentum color (when young): _____ (mature) _____

Indumentum location: _____

Shrub height _____ width _____ , in _____ years

Shrub habit ☐ open; ☐ intermediate; ☐ dense.   leaves held _____ years

Hardy to at least (Specify degrees F or C): Plant _____ Buds _____

Flowering period: ☐ early; ☐ mid; ☐ late   Month: _____

Comments / Other distinguishing features: _____
_____

Photo enclosed: ☐ print; ☐ slide; ☐ electronic; ☐ none.

AMERICAN RHODODENDRON SOCIETY

Instructions for Preparing an Application to Register a Plant Name

Please answer questions as fully as possible. If any requested information is not known, enter "Unknown." Indicate units of length (inch, cm, etc.) and temperature scale (°F, °C) used.

Names must meet the requirements of the *International Code of Nomenclature*, and acceptance is subject to final approval by the International Registrar. A name may consist of not more than 10 syllables and not more than 30 letters or characters overall, excluding spaces. A name that sounds like an existing name should be avoided. A name used previously for a rhododendron or azalea may not be reused.

Shapes: Typical truss, flower, and leaf shapes are illustrated here. Enter appropriate selections on application.

Truss Size and Shape:

Elepidote: measure the height and width of the cluster of flowers from a single bud.

Lepidote or azalea: report the size of the terminal cluster. If more than one bud, report the number of buds per cluster.

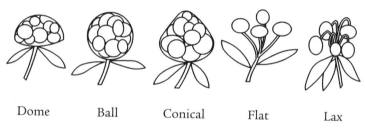

Dome   Ball   Conical   Flat   Lax

Elepidote Trusses

Flower Description: Report basic color of buds and corolla (inside and outside). When prominent, note color variations (margins, throat, midveins, etc.) and color and distribution of spots or blotches. Report also whether the flower ages to a different color. Measure LENGTH of the corolla ALONG the flower from base to tip. See below for Corolla (Flower) shapes.

Leaf Description: If you wish, you may send a typical leaf with your application for the Registrar to describe. Leaf shapes generally fall into one of the following groups:

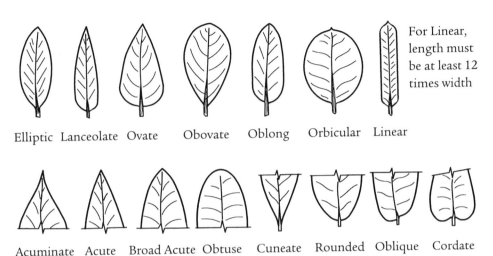

Elliptic Lanceolate Ovate   Obovate   Oblong   Orbicular Linear

For Linear, length must be at least 12 times width

Acuminate Acute Broad Acute Obtuse   Cuneate   Rounded   Oblique   Cordate

Note that the term indumentum refers to scaly as well as hairy covering on the leaves and on other parts. Report type and color of indumentum, whether sparse or heavy, and its location.

While not required, slides or prints are always welcome and are often very helpful supplements to the word description when describing leaf and flowers shapes. Please consider including photos.

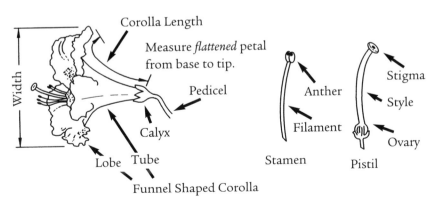

Flower Parts

Corolla Shapes

Several typical corolla shapes are illustrated below. General categories include:

Funnel—rather narrow base with evenly flared tube.

Campanulate—broad, rounded base with essentially parallel-sided tube.

Tubular—narrow or rounded base with narrow, parallel-sided tube.

Actual flowers may exhibit combinations of typical shapes, such as funnel-campanulate. Choose the shape that most closely resembles that of the flower being described.

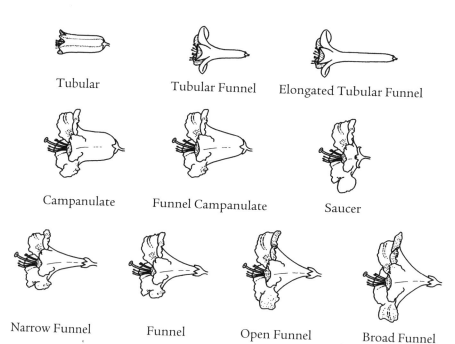

Tubular   Tubular Funnel   Elongated Tubular Funnel

Campanulate   Funnel Campanulate   Saucer

Narrow Funnel   Funnel   Open Funnel   Broad Funnel

Appendix D

U.S. Department of Agriculture Hardiness Zones

Average annual minimum temperature for each hardiness zone

Hardiness zone	°F	°C
1	less than −50	less than −45.5
2	−50 to −40	−45.5 to −40.1
3	−40 to −30	−40.0 to −34.5
4	−30 to −20	−34.4 to −28.9
5	−20 to −10	−28.8 to −23.4
6	−10 to 0	−23.3 to −17.8
7	0 to 10	−17.7 to −12.3
8	10 to 20	−12.2 to −6.7
9	20 to 30	−6.6 to −1.2
10	30 to 40	−1.1 to 4.4
11	more than 40	more than 4.4

Appendix E

Metric Equivalents for English Units

inches × 2.5 = centimeters
feet × 0.3 = meters
miles × 1.6 = kilometers
ounces × 31.1 = grams
teaspoons × 4.9 = milliliters
fluid ounces × 29.5 = milliliters
cups × 0.24 = liters
gallons × 3.8 = liters

$(°F - 32) × 5/9 = °C$
change of 1°F = change of 0.6°C

Bibliography

Argent, G., J. Bond, D. Chamberlain, P. Cox, and A. Hardy. 1997. *The Rhododendron Handbook*. London: The Royal Horticultural Society.

Bowers, C. 2003. *Native Azaleas of the Eastern United States and Their Cultivars*. Pawling, New York: Quaker Hill Native Plant Garden.

Case, F., and R. Case. 1997. *Trilliums*. Portland, Oregon: Timber Press.

Dirr, M. 1997. *Dirr's Hardy Trees and Shrubs*. Portland, Oregon: Timber Press.

Dirr, M. 2002. *Dirr's Shrubs and Trees for Warm Climates*. Portland, Oregon: Timber Press.

Galle, F. 1968. *Native and Some Introduced Azaleas for Southern Gardens*. Booklet 2. Pine Mountain, Georgia: Callaway Gardens.

Galle, F. 1974. *Southern Living Azaleas*. Birmingham, Alabama: Oxmoor House.

Galle, F. 1985. *Azaleas*. Portland, Oregon: Timber Press.

Jaynes, R. A. 1975. *The Laurel Book: Rediscovery of the North American Laurels*. New York: Hafner Press.

Jaynes, R. A. 1988. *Kalmia: The Laurel Book II*. Portland, Oregon: Timber Press.

Jaynes, R. A. 1997. *Mountain Laurel and Related Species*. Portland, Oregon: Timber Press.

Justice, S., and R. Bell. 1968. *Wild Flowers of North Carolina*. Chapel Hill: University of North Carolina Press.

Kron, K. A. 1993. A revision of *Rhododendron* section *Pentanthera. Edinburgh Journal of Botany* 50(3): 249–365.

Kron, K. A., and M. Creel. 1999. A new species of deciduous azalea (*Rhodo-dendron* section *Pentanthera*; Ericaceae) from South Carolina. *Novon: A Journal of Botanical Nomenclature* 9(3): 377–380.

Liberty Hyde Bailey Hortorium. 1976. *Hortus Third*. New York: Macmillan.

Livingston, P., and F. West. 1978. *Hybrids and Hybridizers: Rhododendrons and Azaleas for Eastern North America*. Newtown Square, Pennsylvania: Harrowood Books.

Mossman, F. D. 1977. The western azalea on Stagecoach Hill. *Pacific Horticulture* 38: 28–33.

Radford, R., H. Ahles, and C. Bell. 1968. *Manual of the Vascular Flora of the Carolinas*. Chapel Hill: University of North Carolina Press.

Skinner, H. T. 1955. In search of native azaleas. *Morris Arboretum Bulletin* (Philadelphia) 6: 1–10, 15–22.

Wilson, E. H., and A. Rehder. 1921. *A Monograph of Azaleas*. Arnold Arboretum Publication No. 9. Cambridge, Massachusetts: Harvard University.

Index

Alabama azalea. See *Rhododendron
alabamense*
Allegheny spurge (*Pachysandra
procumbens*), 65
American arborvitae (*Thuja
occidentalis*), 72
American Rhododendron Society,
123, 127
American wisteria (*Wisteria frutescens*),
73
Aromi azaleas, 94
arrowwood (*Viburnum dentatum*), 67
azalea bark scale (*Eriocossus azaleae*),
56
azalea bud larva (*Orthosia hibisci*), 56
azalea caterpillar (*Datana major*), 57
azalea cultivars, 47, 96–106, 121–123
azalea generations, 90
azalea whitefly (*Pealius azalea*), 57
azaleodendrons, 118

bearberry (*Arctostaphylos uva-ursi*), 12,
65
black vine weevil (*Otiorhynchus
sulcatus*), 57
bleeding heart (*Dicentra eximia*), 65
bloodroot (*Sanguinaria canadensis*), 65

bog rosemary (*Andromeda polifolia*), 65
botanical forms and varieties, 18, 28,
29
botanical terms, 18, 29

Carolina cherrylaurel (*Prunus
caroliniana*), 72
Carolina jasmine (*Gelsemium
sempervirens*), 73
catch-fly azalea. See *Rhododendron
viscosum*
Chinese azalea. See *Rhododendron
molle*
chlorosis, 50
Christmas fern (*Polystichum
acrostichoides*), 65
chromosomes, 82, 118
    allotetraploid, 82
    autotetraploid, 82
    diploid, 82, 118
    haploid, 118
    hexaploid, 118
    polyploid, 118
    tetraploid, 82, 118
    triploid, 82, 118
clammy azalea. See *Rhododendron
viscosum*

cliffgreen (*Paxistima canbyi*), 66
coastal azalea. See *Rhododendron atlanticum*
color stability, 48, 110
companion plants, 64–74
Confederate azaleas, 94
Coral bells (*Heuchera sanguinea*), 66
cranberry (*Vaccinium macrocarpon*), 66
crested iris (*Iris cristata*), 66
cross-pollination, 84, 85
crossvine (*Bignonia capreolata*), 73
Cumberland azalea. See *Rhododendron cumberlandense*

deciduous azaleas, 11, 12
distribution ranges, 20, 22, 24, 26, 30
dogwood (*Cornus florida*), 71
drooping leucothoe (*Leucothoë fontanesiana*), 12, 68
dusty zenobia (*Zenobia pulverulenta*), 68

evergreen azaleas, 11, 12
Exbury azaleas, 91

fertilizer, 49, 50, 89, 90
flame azalea. See *Rhododendron calendulaceum*
Florida azalea. See *Rhododendron austrinum*
Florida leucothoe (*Agarista populifolia*), 72
flower traits, 110–114
    apetala, 112
    double, 113
    extra-petal, 112
    picotee, 113
    polypetala, 108, 112
    shapes, 111, 112
    types, 112
foamflower (*Tiarella cordifolia*), 66
foliage, 114, 115
fragrance, 110

fringetree (*Chionanthus virginicus*), 68

genetics, 82
Ghent azaleas, 91
glaciation, 37
growth habits, 115–117
    compact, 116
    fastigiate, 116
    prostrate, 116
    tree azaleas, 117

hardiness zones, 137
hybrid azaleas, 35, 36, 119, 120

Ilam azaleas, 91
inkberry (*Ilex glabra*), 72

Japanese azalea. See *Rhododendron japonicum*

Knap Hill azaleas, 91

lacebug (*Staphinitis pyriodes*), 57
Lazy K azaleas, 94
leaf color, 114
leaf gall (*Exobasidium vaccinii*), 58
leaf miner (*Caloptilia azaleella*), 57
leaf rust (*Puccinniastrum myrtilii*), 58
leaf texture, 115
lingonberry (*Vaccinium vitis-idaea*), 66

Maid in the Shade azaleas, 95
May white azalea. See *Rhododendron eastmanii*
mayflower (*Epigaea repens*), 67
Mollis azaleas, 91
mountain laurel (*Kalmia latifolia*), 42, 68
mountain pieris (*Pieris floribunda*), 68
mulching, 53
ninebark (*Physocarpus opulifolius*), 68

Northern Lights azaleas, 95

oakleaf hydrangea (*Hydrangea quercifolia*), 68
Oconee azalea. See *Rhododendron flammeum*
Oconee bells (*Shortia galacifolia*), 67

Pastel azaleas, 95
Pentanthera, 13–15
petal blight (*Ovulina azaleae*), 58
petiole color, 115
piedmont azalea. See *Rhododendron canescens*
pinkshell azalea. See *Rhododendron vaseyi*
Pinxterbloom azalea. See *Rhododendron periclymenoides*
planting, 50–53
plumleaf azalea. See *Rhododendron prunifolium*
pollen, 83
Pontic azalea. See *Rhododendron luteum*
powdery mildew (*Microsphaea penicillate*), 58
propagation, 79–86
    alternative method, 79–81
    asexual, 75–80
    division, 77
    layering, 77–80
    micropropagation, 80
    rooting cuttings, 76, 77
    sexual, 81–86
pruning, 54, 55

reciprocal crosses, 109
red buckeye (*Aesculus pavia*), 71
redbud (*Cercis canadensis*), 71
red cedar (*Juniperus virginiana*), 72
Rhododendron alabamense, 14, 25, 26, 32, 33, 35
Rhododendron arborescens, 14, 25–28, 31, 34, 37, 42
    (var. *georgiana*), 18, 28, 32

(var. *richardsonii*), 28
Rhododendron atlanticum, 14, 25–27
Rhododendron austrinum, 14, 29, 30
Rhododendron bakeri, 14, 18
Rhododendron calendulaceum, 14, 18, 29–31, 42
Rhododendron canadense, 14, 21, 22, 36
Rhododendron canescens, 14, 23–27, 31, 33
Rhododendron coryi, 29
Rhododendron cumberlandense, 14, 28, 29–31, 37
Rhododendron eastmanii, 32–35
Rhododendron flammeum, 14, 18, 29–31
Rhododendron japonicum, 14, 21
Rhododendron luteum, 14
Rhododendron molle, 14, 21
Rhododendron nudiflorum, 18
Rhododendron oblongifolium, 29
Rhododendron occidentale, 14, 19, 20, 36, 39
Rhododendron periclymenoides, 14, 18, 23, 24, 34, 42
Rhododendron prinophyllum, 14, 18, 23–25, 42
Rhododendron prunifolium, 14, 18, 29–31
Rhododendron roseum, 18, 42
Rhododendron serrulatum, 29
Rhododendron speciosum, 17
Rhododendron vaseyi, 14, 21, 22, 36
Rhododendron viscosum, 14, 25, 26, 28, 34
    (var. *aemulans*), 29
    (var. *montanum*), 28
    (var. *oblongifolium*), 29, 35
    (var. *serrulatum*), 29
RHS Colour Chart, 124
root rot (*Phytophthera cinnamomi*), 58
rosebay rhododendron (*Rhododendron maximum*), 42, 43, 69

roseshell azalea. See *Rhododendron prinophyllum*
Royal Horticultural Society, 13, 123

sandmyrtle (*Leiophyllum buxifolium*), 69
seeds and seed germination, 85–89
serviceberry (*Amelanchier arborea*), 71
sheep laurel (*Kalmia angustifolia*), 69
silverbell (*Halesia tetraptera*), 71
smooth azalea. See *Rhododendron arborescens*
smooth cypress (*Cupressus glabra*), 72
smooth hydrangea (*Hydrangea arborescens*), 69
soil pH, 49
sourwood (*Oxydendrum arboreum*), 71
southern magnolia (*Magnolia grandiflora*), 73
southern red mite (*Oligonychus ilicis*), 57
stem borer (*Obera myops*), 57
Summer azaleas, 95
summersweet (*Clethra alnifolia*), 69
swamp azalea. See *Rhododendron viscosum*
sweet azalea. See *Rhododendron arborescens*
sweetbells (*Leucothoë racemosa*), 70
sweetshrub (*Calycanthus floridus*), 70

sweetspire (*Itea virginica*), 70

trait inheritance, 108, 109
transplanting, 55, 56, 89
trumpet creeper (*Campsis radicans*), 74
trumpet honeysuckle (*Lonicera sempervirens*), 74
Tsutsutsi, 13, 15, 118

variegated foliage, 115
virgin's bower (*Clematis virginiana*), 74
Virginia creeper (*Parthenocissus quinquefolia*), 74

wakerobin (*Trillium erectum*), 67
wandflower (*Galax urceolata*), 67
watering, 53, 54
western azalea. See *Rhododendron occidentale*
white cedar (*Chamaecyparis thyoides*), 73
wild ginger (*Asarum shuttleworthii*), 67
winterberry (*Ilex verticillata*), 70
wintergreen (*Gaultheria procumbens*), 67
witch alder (*Fothergilla major*), 70
wood vamp (*Decumaria barbara*), 74

yellowroot (*Xanthorhiza simplicissima*), 70